SMOCKING

SMOCKING

Audrey Vincente Dean

STANLEY PAUL
London Melbourne Sydney Auckland Johannesburg

With love to my mother, who encouraged me so much

Stanley Paul & Co. Ltd
An imprint of the Hutchinson Publishing Group
17–21 Conway Street, London W1P 6JD

Hutchinson Group (Australia) Pty Ltd
30–32 Cremorne Street, Richmond South, Victoria 3121
PO Box 151, Broadway, New South Wales 2007

Hutchinson Group (NZ) Ltd
32–34 View Road, PO Box 40-086, Glenfield, Auckland 10

Hutchinson Group (SA) Pty Ltd
PO Box 337, Bergvlei 2012, South Africa

First published 1983
© Audrey Vincente Dean 1983

Set in Linotron Baskerville by
A-Line Services, Saffron Walden, Essex

Printed in Great Britain by the Anchor Press Ltd,
and bound by Wm Brendon & Son Ltd,
both of Tiptree, Essex

British Library Cataloguing in Publication Data
Dean, Audrey Vincente
Smocking.
1. Smocking.
I. Title
746.44   TT840

ISBN 0 09 150201 2

CONTENTS

Chapter Four   Children's Patterns

Chapter Five   Adults' Patterns

Chapter Six   Patterns Using Canadian or Ruched Smocking

Chapter Seven   Novelties and Ideas

INTRODUCTION

The type of needlework known as smocking is ancient in origin. In the sixteenth century the neckbands and sleeves of men's shirts were heavily embroidered in this way. Ladies' shifts or chemises, which were undergarments showing at the neck and sleeves, also displayed rich needlework on the gathers.

The decoration continued until the eighteenth century, when there was a change. Waistbands rose, dresses became more clinging round the upper body, and chemises did not suit the fashions. Gentlemen's shirts were simplified in cut. Smocking was now applied to countrymen's outer garments, where it served the practical purpose of shaping the width of material, needed to cover the lower body, into the narrower bodice at the front and back. The smock, as it was called, provided ease of movement, warmth through its gathered folds, and durability which justified the amount of work lavished on it. Its ornament could also be varied to suit the personal preference of the wearer without becoming bizarre in any way. It is not surprising that its popularity continued until well into the nineteenth century.

Smocks were made of heavy cotton or linen, which was mostly left in its natural colour or very occasionally dyed brown or indigo blue. Sunday smocks were always pure white and were often given as a love-token from a future bride to her groom, to be worn at their wedding. The stitchery was worked in colours which matched the material. Emphasis was placed on the texture created by the stitches with their many rows of repetition, rather than on the formation of linear patterns. On either side of the smocking were bands of mainly geometrically-patterned stitchery, worked in chain and feather stitches interspersed with French knots, which sometimes denoted the trade of the wearer by symbolic motifs.

England is not the only country where a tradition of smocking exists. Rich peasant embroidery is still found in such countries as Norway, Switzerland and Yugoslavia, while in Spain there are country-women's smocked skirts, blue smocked blouses for boys and short decorative shirts for men.

1
PREPARATION

FABRICS

The function of smocking on the peasant garment was to hold the gathers in place and to give elasticity to the fit, and that remains its primary use today; but because smocking is so decorative it is sometimes worked on inset bands for purely ornamental effect.

The easiest types of material to smock are smooth and even. Do not attempt to work anything with a bouclé or 'hairy' surface. You should also avoid any fabric with a springy or crease-resisting texture as it can be difficult to draw up into regular gathers. Medium weights, such as cotton, wool and cotton mixtures, silk or fine wool, are easiest for a beginner. Fine single jersey also smocks well. Light material such as chiffon or nylon looks delightful when smocked, but needs more practice as fine embroidery thread and complete accuracy in placing the stitches are vital. The delicate effect is lost if the smocking is not worked very neatly.

Heavier weaves, such as velvet, needlecord, double jersey or the traditional linen can give a handsome and striking effect, but it is essential to have deep pleats.

Bold and unusual results come from smocking such fabrics as denim, hessian or felt, though with these, as well as gathering the pleats deeply, you must match the weight of the embroidery threads to the material. Try embroidery wool or cotton used double. Knitting wool or plastic raffia would give an unusual appearance.

As a rough guide the fabric should measure three times the required finished length of smocking, but this will vary according to the space between the dots, which embroidery stitches are used and how firmly the embroideress works. As in knitting or crochet tension varies greatly from person to person. The aim should be to achieve evenness; this is not difficult as the action of smocking is very rhythmical.

PREPARING THE FABRIC WITH TRANSFERRED DOTS

Although the effect of smocking can be rich and complicated the embroidery stitches are simple and easy to learn. The basis of the work is the gathering stitches which when pulled up form straight and uniform tubes or pleats. To ensure their regularity the placing of the gathering stitches must be absolutely accurate. The 'tubes' are created by pulling these regularly spaced stitches closer together. Each gathering thread must be pulled to a precise tension to create perfect regularity.

The most usual way of spacing these gathers is by ironing sheets of dotted transfers onto the wrong side of the material. The transfers are available in sheets about 20 cm (8 in) wide by 75 cm (30 in) long, and can be bought in needlework shops. If you need a larger area of gathering it is much more accurate to join transfers together on the back by gluing or using sticky tape before ironing off, rather than by trying to place the extra bits correctly on the material.

You may be asked when buying transfers what spacing you need. The sizes most often used have the dots placed 6 or 8 mm (¼ or ⅜ in) apart, and sometimes these are the only transfers available. Fine- and medium-weight materials can be worked by these spacings, but with any heavier weights you will have to pick up every second or third dot only to give deeper pleats. If you are in doubt experiment on a small piece, and if the drawn-up threads do not give firm and well-defined gathers, use a wider spacing of dots.

Because fine materials like nylon will gather up so much more closely than a medium-weight cotton you will find that a width of smocking takes up more material than three times its measurement. This may or may not be acceptable, but if it is not, use a transfer with dots more closely spaced than 6–8 mm (¼–⅜ in). There will be more gathers and shallower pleats than with the larger spacing, so that less material is thus needed.

After any necessary experiments the transfer should be trimmed or added to, so that the correct number of dots can be printed. The amount of dots and rows needed for each design is given in this book. In all cases one more dot is transferred than the number of pleats required for the pattern; the extra stitch on this dot is required to finish the last pleat.

Smocking is easier to embroider if you gather one extra row at the top and bottom of the piece so that the first and last rows of embroidery have firmly held material above and below them. Do not transfer an extra row at the bottom when using semi-transparent material as the dots will show through when the gathering threads are withdrawn.

When designing your own pattern you will need to work a trial piece first. The number of pleats in a repeat, rather than the number of stitches, needs to be carefully counted. For instance, a wave of six stitches up and six down will take twelve pleats over each repeat, plus another two pleats to complete the pattern at the end. All the other stitch repeats which are used in combination with the main pattern will have to fit in with the total number of pleats you are going to use. This is not difficult as smaller stitches take less pleats per repeat and so they are more simple to arrange. It is not advisable to iron off enough dots to cover an area of material, gather them and then try to work out a pattern which will fit without any preliminary planning.

With the correct transfer size to hand you are ready to begin. Overstitch the top edge of the material if it tends to fray too much. If possible pull a thread about 2 cm (¾ in) parallel to the top edge to give a guide that will ensure that the dots lie along the straight grain of the material. Place an ironing pad on a flat surface at least as large as the area which is to be transferred and smooth the uncreased material over it with the wrong side facing you. Cut the manufacturer's name away from the paper and keep it for a test piece. Place the upper edge of the paper level with the pulled thread or the straight edge of material so that the top line of dots comes not less than 12 mm (½ in) below. Alternatively you may place the top line of dots just below the raw edge itself. Directions are given in the patterns included in this book. Carefully stick pins through the paper and the material into the ironing pad, so that the transfer is firmly fixed. Make sure that its inked side is against the fabric. The dots on the inked side will be slightly raised or will be clearer than on the reverse.

Heat the iron to the cotton setting, and as a test try stamping the manufacturer's name on to a spare bit of fabric. You will then discover how long you need to press the iron on the paper for the best results.

Some transfers are printed with yellow dots for use on dark materials, but if these are unobtainable you can tack a blue transfer in place and gather through the paper. Tear it away afterwards. Yellow dots are sometimes used on transparent fabric.

Be especially careful with multi-print transfers which can iron off so heavily that they seep straight through fine fabrics and can even mark the right side of thicker ones.

PREPARING THE FABRIC BY OTHER METHODS

It is possible to gather material without transferred dots if it has regular markings printed or in the weave, such as checks, spots, stripes or crinkly seersucker bands.

Checks

A small gingham check of 6 mm (¼ in) is one of the easiest to smock. This means that there will be four dark squares and four light squares to every 2.5 cm (1 in) in the pattern row. Pick up the light squares, in at the bottom right and out at the left-hand corners, on every other row of checks. When the gathering threads are drawn up the dark squares only will show. For a light background to the smocking pick up the dark squares. On this size of check a fine gather will result. On a larger pattern pick up a few threads at the corners only of the squares, adjusting your pattern so that the gathering stitches are 6–12 mm (¼–½ in) away from one another.

Spots

Spots are woven or printed to lie under one another in alternate rows. If possible choose material where the spots are 6–12 mm (¼–½ in) apart. Pick up the spots as though they were transferred dots, using alternate rows. On a patterned material of a larger scale adjust the stitches as for checks, taking perhaps the centre of each spot and the centre of each space between them as the fabric allows. Gather on the wrong side of the material.

Stripes

Again it is easier to use a small-scale pattern which allows the stitches to be placed 6–12 mm (¼–½ in) apart. You will need to rule faint pencil lines on the wrong side of the material to guide the gathering, 6 mm–2 cm (¼–¾ in) apart. As for checked material, pick up the middle of the light stripe if the smocking is to appear on a dark area, or the middle of a dark stripe for a light background.

Seersucker bands

You may pick up either every plain or every crinkled band for a very full gathering, or place a stitch in the centre of each if you wish to use only half the amount of material. Test gather a small piece first.

Other ways of making dots

If you cannot obtain a smocking transfer which you need for plain fabric, you may mark in the dots yourself, using one of the following methods:

Graph paper and carbon Place a sheet of carbon paper face downwards on the fabric. Try to use embroidery carbon from a needlework shop, as this does not transfer accidental hand pressure and so on. Place graph paper or a hand-ruled grid above it. Pin the layers together and place them on a hard surface – glass is the best. It is easy to make pits in a polished table. Mark in dots with a hard pencil.

Ruled grid Mark in dots with HB pencil or washable embroidery pencil, using a ruler. Do not use felt pen; it will smudge and marks may be permanent. Pull a thread to guide the top line.

Template This can be used several times. Rule a grid on thin card and push holes through it at the intersections with a large needle. These may be enlarged with a fine knitting needle. Mark dots through the holes, moving the template along as required.

GATHERING AND PULLING UP THE THREADS

Choose strong thread in a contrasting colour to the fabric. This will serve as a clear guide when you are working the embroidery.

Cut a length equal to one row plus a few centimetres (more if rows are shorter than 30 cm (12 in) to save constant rethreading of the needle). On heavy material it is advisable to use double threads as nothing is more tiresome than to have the gathering break when you are pulling it up.

Make a large knot on the end, and pick up each dot only if working on medium- or light-weight material. To help the pleats stay in place on heavier material it is helpful to pick up two or three threads on either side of the dot. The thread will then run through the centre of the resulting gathers.

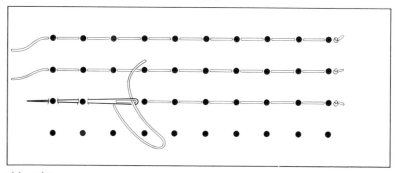

pick up dots

Figure 1

Leave 5–7.5 cm (2–3 in) of thread hanging at the end of each row of gathering. When all are complete pull them up in pairs. You may knot them together to secure when drawn up if the smocking area is small. Cut off the excess to within 2–4 cm (1–1½ in). Alternatively, wind them criss-cross round a pin inserted at right angles to each pair of gathering rows, and cut off the excess when the winding is firm. The pin method is preferable as it allows the gathers to be adjusted if necessary.

When the threads are all pulled up the tubes or pleats of material on the right side should touch each other and be perfectly regular, without being crushed together. It is difficult to work smocking on gathers which have not been sufficiently drawn up. On a large piece the tubes may not always stay perfectly in place along their length, although the preparatory rows may have been put in perfectly accurately. Try drawing up one or two threads a little more where they seem disarranged. Here is the advantage of the pin method. As you work the

pulled up gathers wrong side

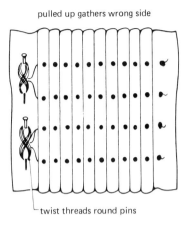

twist threads round pins

Figure 2

smocking the even tension of the stitches will often regularize the
pleats so that the finished work will appear even.

When drawing up a large area of gathers it is sometimes
difficult to draw up each set of threads uniformly. It will be
found helpful to pin the right-hand or knotted straight edge of
the piece to an ironing board with dressmaker's pins to provide a
firm base when pulling up the threads. Check the width of the
total number of gathers with a ruler to make sure they remain
the same across the length.

ADAPTING PATTERNS FOR SMOCKING

Patterns for smocked clothes, mostly for babies and small
children, are available, but often the choice is very limited, and
sometimes insufficient material is allowed to form correct
gathers. It is quite easy to adapt other patterns to incorporate
smocking, and sometimes a pattern can be taken from an
existing garment which fits well. The added elasticity given by
the work will ensure allowance for growth.

Dresses for young children often have the front part of the
bodice smocked. The embroidery may be worked over a straight
centre panel between the armholes, starting 2.5–5 cm (1–2 in)
away from them on either side and reaching down to the waist
and up to the neck. If preferred the smocking may cover all the
front bodice area between the side seams with the armholes cut

out of the smocked area. Sometimes the gathers are set into a straight yoke which reaches 7.5–10 cm (3–4 in) below the neck.

(b) set into straight yoke

(a) straight centre panel

(c) all the front bodice area

Figure 3

Whichever style you choose, the smocking should always be worked before the dress is cut out and sewn. Decide first on the size of the smocked panel. The easiest way to do this is to take measurements from a dress which fits well, while it is worn. You will be able to visualize the smocking and make any necessary adjustments to its placing. Insert a few pins to mark the area.

Decide on the smocking pattern and the number of dots and rows which will give the required amount of smocking. Alter the transfer if necessary and position it on the material allowing sufficient surplus for seams on either side. Work the smocking and withdraw the gathering threads. Place the dress pattern on the embroidered material, being careful to position the centre of

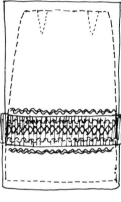

set strip of smocking between
two pieces of material

Figure 4

the pattern on the centre pleat. Make sure the pattern centre lies on the same pleat for the entire length of the smocking. Tack round the outline, machine over tacking and then cut out like any other material.

Patterns for adult clothes can be made up in the same way. If the panel of smocking is to be inset it should be stitched into position between strips of material large enough to accommodate the pattern piece before the cutting out is fully complete.

SMOCKING CIRCULAR NECKLINES

Smocking looks very attractive when worked on a round-necked peasant style of dress or blouse. Circular smocking can also surround a plain centre set into the middle of the embroidery.

The pieces of material embroidered are straight, and the curve results from the choice of smocking stitches, which are arranged so that the fullness is gathered in at one edge and released at the other. In the case of peasant necklines a small narrow hem and a drawstring run along the gathered edge to make it firmer, or it may be bound. Lingerie styles may allow the neckline edge to escape in an attractive frill.

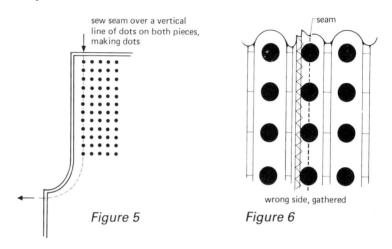

Figure 5   *Figure 6*

A certain amount of making up is necessary before the embroidery is worked. The dots are transferred up to or over the seam allowance and the raw edges may need slight adjustment to allow the seams to be sewn over a vertical line of matched dots on adjoining pieces. In this way you will ensure that the dots come at the bottom of the gathers on the right side and remain invisible. Count the dots to make sure you will have the right number of pleats before joining the seams as it will be impossible to adjust them later. When putting in the gathering threads start and finish each pair in a different place. This will help to ensure that the prepared tubes are smooth and even. Knot each drawn-up pair of threads together instead of twisting them round a pin which would get in the way of the embroidery.

CARE OF SMOCKING

Smocking is remarkably hard-wearing and will not lose its elasticity. When you have finished the embroidery and withdrawn the gathering threads it may be helpful, particularly if you are working on a fairly heavy material, to set it in place by holding a steam iron a little way above the surface on the wrong side, and allowing the steam to play over the area. Alternatively, use a damp cloth and an ordinary iron. You should never place the weight of the iron on the gathers. If necessary you may slightly stretch the smocking sideways by this method.

Hand wash smocked garments as though they were woollens by squeezing up and down in warm water. Do not rub. Allow to drip dry, then iron only up to the gathered area, which will not need attention. The smocking will not crush when the garment is worn.

CHOOSING THE THREAD AND NEEDLES

It is important to match the weight and texture of the embroidery thread to the material. It must make the stitches show up well by its texture and thickness as well as by its colour.

Stranded cotton is the most readily available embroidery thread. Use four strands in a crewel needle and save the two extra strands for use with two more surplus strands of the same length. Combine it with fine- and medium-weight cottons, fine wool and wool and cotton mixtures. On nylon you may need only three strands in the needle to combine with the fine gathers.

Soft embroidery cotton thread in a chenille needle gives a bold and striking effect for use with thicker fabrics such as linen or heavy cotton. A chenille needle is short and thick with a large eye. Crewel needles come in different sizes, like sewing needles, and have long eyes.

Wool tapestry thread looks well with jersey or medium-weight wool. Use a chenille needle.

Pearl cotton and *coton à broder* are available in two unstranded thicknesses, and may be used on medium-weight materials and on velvet, with crewel needles.

For special effects, particularly on more loosely woven materials, try knitting wool, plastic raffia or crochet thread.

As it has to withstand being constantly pulled through the material the thread must be smooth and fairly strong. Make sure the eye of the needle is sufficiently large to part the fabric enough to allow the folded double end of the thread to pass through without too much tugging.

STARTING AND FINISHING OFF

In a smocking pattern it is essential to have the largest motif centred in the middle of an area. Count to the centre pleat and mark this with a coloured thread, which will be useful when you come to make up the smocking. Begin by working the main motif from the centre to the right-hand side. Turn the work upside down and embroider from the centre to the other side, keeping the continuity of the design. This makes sure that the pattern will finish at the same point in the repeat on either side. Once the sequence is established the work can start in the usual way from the beginning of the row.

It may be tempting to cut a long thread, more than 40 cm (16 in) to avoid having to finish off too often, but you run a greater risk of tangling it and it often becomes tired and frayed towards the end.

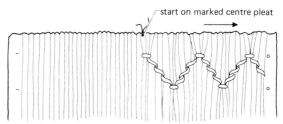

Figure 7

Start with a double knot. To finish off, come through to the wrong side and work one or two back stitches on top of a pleat. Continue the row by bringing the needle through in exactly the same place as you finished off.

It is not essential to fasten off at the end of a row if you are continuing the stitching in the same colour. Turn the smocking upside down and continue from the same side, working in the opposite direction.

Loops running up and down the pleats at the back of the work are permissible, but make sure that any crossing them are less than 12 mm (½ in) long. The elasticity of the smocking will be spoiled, and it is better to end off and start again in the next section.

The stitches should be set into the pleats halfway between their tops and the gathering thread. Do not pull them too tightly when working. Practise to achieve a neat and even appearance.

2
STITCHES

REPEATED STITCHES

The stitches which stretch well are the diamond and all the honeycombs such as surface honeycomb, honeycomb and van-dyke stitches.

Those which do not stretch so well are outline and cable, wave and trellis patterns, with their variations.

Outline stitch

This stitch and cable stitch are often used along the first row of gathers to hold them firmly in place. They also define the pattern by their straight lines. Work from left to right. Bring the needle up in the first pleat, and set it into the next pleat in a slanting position which should be the same for every stitch. Keep the thread below the needle.

Figure 8

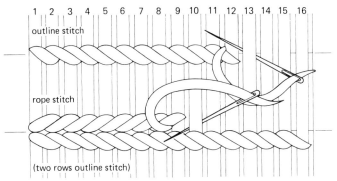

Figure 9

Rope stitch

This is two rows of outline stitches which mirror each other. Keep the thread below the needle for the upper row and above the needle for the lower row. The rows may touch, or there may be a slight space between them.

Single cable stitch

Work from left to right. Bring the needle up in the first pleat, set it horizontally into the second pleat with the thread below the needle and catch these two pleats together. Set the needle horizontally into the third pleat on the same level as the first stitch, but with the thread above the needle, and catch the second and third pleats together. Continue in this way, advancing one pleat with every stitch, the thread being alternately below and above the needle.

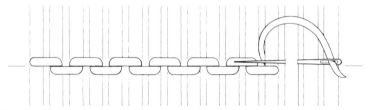

Figure 10

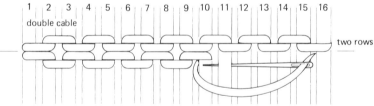

Figure 11

Double cable stitch

Work two rows of cable stitch touching each other. Place the upper-thread stitch of the lower row next to the lower-thread stitch of the upper row, so as to resemble links of a chain.

Basket stitch

This is an extension of double cable and is worked in the same way, so that every row, except the first and last, has the stitches pairing off. Continue to fill the shape required. It gives a solid appearance and can be used to resemble the weaving on a basket of flowers motif, the flowers suggested by detached chain stitches.

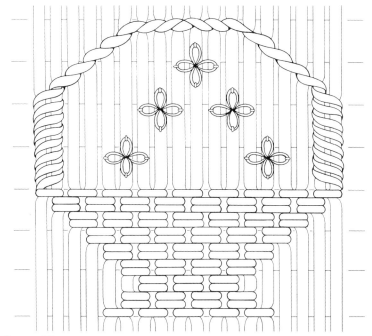

Figure 12

Figure 12 shows a flower basket which may be repeated as the main motif of a design. It occupies seventeen pleats and seven spaces between eight gathering threads. Begin on the fifth gathering thread with seventeen cable stitches. Continue as shown having two less cable stitches on each successive row until on the seventh row there are seven. For the 'foot' of the basket work another row of seven, and a final row of nine. Shape the handle with stem stitches and fill in the space under the handle with chain stitch flowerettes and leaves as described on p. 31.

Diamond stitch

This is worked from left to right. Several rows worked together give a very pretty effect. Start in the first pleat, on the lower of two gathering threads.

Stitch 1 Set the needle horizontally into the second pleat with the thread below the needle.

Stitch 2 Take a horizontal stitch into the third pleat on the level of the upper gathering thread with the thread below the needle.

Stitch 3 Now with thread above the needle take a horizontal top-level stitch into the fourth pleat.

Stitch 4 With the thread still above the needle go back to the lower gathering thread and take a horizontal stitch into the fifth pleat. This comprises one unit. Repeat the units over each group of four pleats, remembering to progress one pleat on each stitch.

Paired diamond stitch

This is worked in the same way as the single diamond, except that the rows are worked with the upper and lower stitches pairing off, as in the double cable stitch.

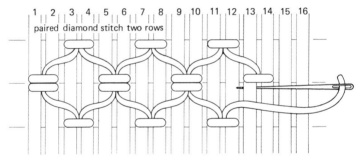

Figure 13

Crossed diamond stitch

Two colours look well in this stitch. Embroider one row of diamond stitch, then work a second row over the first one, by taking together the pleats missed in the first row. See the little girl's pinafore dress on p. 60.

Wave stitch

Work from left to right. To work upwards bring up the thread in the first pleat on a level with the lower gathering thread. Set the needle horizontally into the second pleat with the thread below the needle. Take a stitch into the third pleat, and two more in the fourth and fifth pleats, each slightly higher than the previous stitch and having the thread below the needle in each case. This completes the upward slope and can be increased or decreased as you wish, ending level with one or more gathering threads above the one where you started.

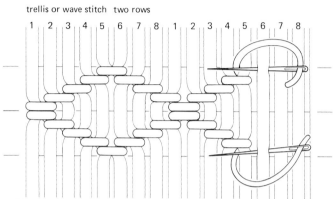

trellis or wave stitch two rows

Figure 14

On the downward slope, take a stitch in the sixth pleat on the same level as the last stitch, with the thread above the needle, and progress downwards for three more stitches, making each correspond with those in the upward slope. One unit is now complete and is repeated in each group of eight pleats for this size of wave, advancing one pleat with every stitch.

When calculating how many pleats will be needed for repeats of this stitch you should multiply the number of stitches up and down in each wave by the number of repeats and add two pleats, because one is unshared at the beginning and one at the end. In this example four stitches up and four down make eight stitches; to repeat it five times you need forty pleats, plus the extra two, totalling forty-two pleats in all.

Double or triple wave stitch

One row of wave stitch is seldom seen on its own. It is more usual to work another one or two rows fitting into the zigzags, either spaced or close together. See the skirt with tapered back and front panels on p. 99.

Trellis stitch

Work one row of wave stitch as shown in Figure 14. Then work another row pairing with it, having the zigzags pointing in the opposite direction. The upper and lower stitches of the two rows

should touch. See the baby's angel top on p. 39. Double or triple
wave stitch rows can also be made into trellis stitch.

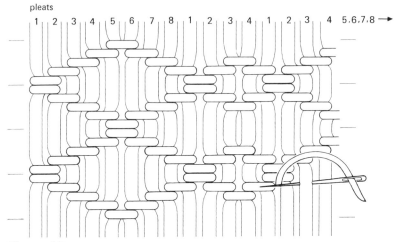

Figure 15

Trellis stitch variation

The number of pleats used in this varies on alternate trellises.
Make sure you end the row with the same size which began it, for
symmetry. See the baby's dress with straight yoke on p. 52.

Honeycomb stitch

This stitch and the two following ones draw the gathers into a
cell effect. Very little of the embroidery thread is seen in
honeycomb, so that it can be worked in a matching thread for
purely textural effects. It is worked from left to right. Come up to
the left of the first pleat, in a line with the upper gathering

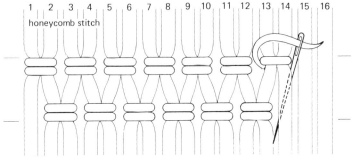

Figure 16

thread. Take a level stitch through the first and second pleats, catch these together with a second stitch, this time slipping the needle down the back of the second pleat until the lower gathering thread is reached, then bring it up. Catch the second and third pleats together with a level stitch, make another stitch over this and slip the needle up the back of the third pleat to the level of the upper gathering thread. Carry on up and down the row. The next row is worked the same as the upper one, over the next pair of gathering threads below.

Surface honeycomb stitch

Work from left to right. Bring the needle out on the top row of gathering in the first pleat. Set it horizontally into the second pleat with the thread above, and with the thread still above set the needle into the same pleat on the lower level. With the thread below the needle take a horizontal stitch into the third pleat on the lower level; still keeping the thread below, set the needle horizontally through the same pleat at top level.

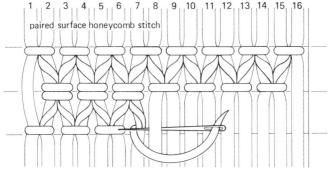

Figure 17

For the second row, work in the same direction, beginning at the first pleat on a lower level and pairing with the first row. The stitch forms diamond shapes like diamond stitch, except that there are no pleats left free in the centres of the diamonds.

Vandyke stitch

This is worked, unusually, from right to left and is similar in effect to surface honeycomb, except that the threads surrounding the cells are more evident. Bring up the needle in the second pleat from the right-hand side, on the lower gathering thread.

Work a horizontal back stitch over the first two pleats. Go up to
the upper gathering thread, set the needle horizontally through
the second and third pleats together and make a back stitch over
them. Go down to the lower gathering thread and work as
before, with the third and fourth tubes. Continue in this way to
the left-hand side of the work.

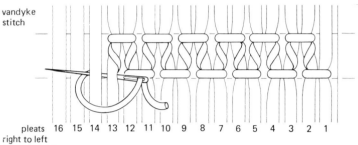

vandyke stitch

pleats   16 15 14 13 12 11 10 9 8 7 6 5 4 3 2 1
right to left

Figure 18

Vandyke stitch, two rows

Work as for the upper row, starting so that the top stitch pairs
with the lower stitch of the top row.

Double vandyke stitch

This is again worked from right to left, and may be used to finish
off a pattern. Bring the needle up in the second pleat, set it
horizontally through the first and second pleats together and
take a back stitch, come down to the next gathering thread, take
the second and third pleats together and back stitch over, then

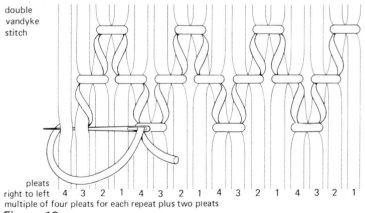

double vandyke stitch

pleats
right to left   4 3 2 1   4 3 2 1   4 3 2 1   4 3 2 1
multiple of four pleats for each repeat plus two pleats

Figure 19

go down to the third gathering thread and take a back stitch over, for the lowest stitch. Go up to the second gathering thread and take the fourth and fifth pleats together with a back stitch over, then up to the first gathering thread to take fifth and sixth pleats together, with a back stitch over. Continue up and down to the end of the row. The second row is worked to pair with the first.

Feather stitch

This is also worked from right to left. Come up on the right of the first pleat level with the lower gathering thread. Insert the needle just below the place where you came up and take a horizontal stitch through pleats 1 and 2, thus making a loop round the needle. Continue, advancing one pleat at every stitch. *Take the second stitch, keeping the needle horizontal, slightly above

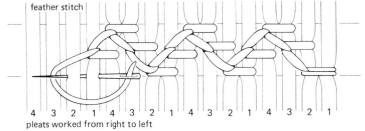

feather stitch

4 3 2 1 4 3 2 1 4 3 2 1 4 3 2 1
pleats worked from right to left

Figure 20

halfway between the lower and upper gathering threads, and the third stitch on a level with the upper gathering thread. The fourth stitch is placed slightly below halfway between the two threads and the fifth on a level with the lower thread. Repeat from*, keeping the thread always below the needle.

DECORATIVE STITCHES FOR ISOLATED USE

Spool stitch

This might also be called 'column stitch'. Come up from the left-hand side of where you are placing the decoration, and taking between two and four pleats together make horizontal stitches, one on top of the other, from right to left, until the desired space is filled.

Flowerettes

These are made from small detached groups of stitches, and look pretty in the middle of trellises.

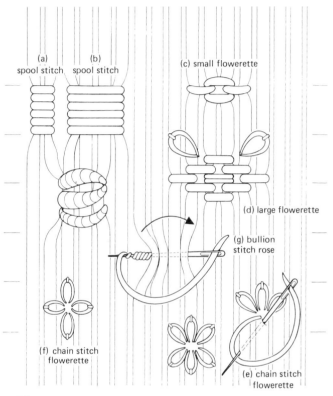

Figure 21

Small flowerette   Each of these occupies four pleats. Take three cable stitches with the thread alternately below and above the needle; then from the end of the third stitch go underneath and come up again on the left of the second pleat, and take another level stitch with the thread below the needle. Take the needle to the wrong side to finish off.

Large flowerette   This is really a small individual trellis and takes six pleats. Starting at the left, come up in the first pleat, set the needle horizontally on the same level into the second pleat with the thread below; take one horizontal stitch a little higher into the third pleat, again with the thread below. Take a third horizontal stitch in the fourth pleat for the top of the trellis, with the thread above the needle and with the thread again above come down a little to take a stitch in the fifth pleat. A horizontal stitch on the same level in the sixth pleat completes the top half of the trellis. Work the lower half to correspond; then fill in the centre in another colour with two stitches over the two centre pleats, one over the other. These two flowerettes may have small surrounding leaves worked by taking detached chain stitch over two pleats.

Chain stitch flowerette This is worked by taking four or six detached chain stitches, the top and bottom ones over the same two pleats, and the side ones over two pleats each, so that this decoration takes up three pleats.

Bullion stitch roses Three bullion stitches, like elongated French knots over four pleats, make delightful roses, though more patience is needed in mastering the stitch. Work one on top of the other, and add one or two detached chain stitches for tiny leaves, over two pleats each. Bring the needle out in the first left-hand pleat, then insert it horizontally four pleats to the right to pick up a back stitch, but do not pull the needle right through the fabric. Wind the thread seven or eight times around the needle close to where it emerges from the material, making sure this is the thick part of the needle. Place the thumb lightly upon the coils and pull the thread through. Still holding the coiled thread turn the needle back to where it was inserted, and push it to the back through the same place. This makes one bullion knot, which should resemble a tiny curved caterpillar on the surface of the material. Adjust by making more or less coils on the needle. Bring the needle out again in the first pleat for each successive stitch.

3
A Few Other Details

HOW TO USE THE SMOCKING DIAGRAMS IN THIS BOOK

The stitch designs shown here are in many cases interchangeable. It is not necessary to keep to the one suggested for the article you would like to make. Many of them are centred by the method suggested on p. 20, so that you do not need to calculate the exact number of pleats needed. If necessary they can easily be altered in depth by repeating or omitting sections. For instance, the baby's dress with a straight yoke may have the small trellis in the centre repeated as in the pockets.

DESIGNING YOUR OWN SMOCKING PATTERNS

'Design your own patterns' are words which bring a chill to most people, yet it often comes about quite naturally that as you become more experienced you put more of your own ideas into your work until you are inventing your own designs.

You can often save yourself a lot of time if you work a small sample first to try out ideas and colour schemes. Aim at a pleasant combination of the different outlines of the stitches; zigzag trellis being steadied by straight lines, and so on. Do not use too many completely different stitches in the same design. The effect will be restless and fussy, and if you try to cram too many stitches into the area to be smocked the work will be stiff and tight, cutting down on its elasticity. Spaces as well as stitches are part of the design.

A simple formula to follow is to start with an outline stitch such as cable, work a more open section using diagonal lines and then a straight-line section only about half as wide, with perhaps the same outline stitch on either side. Leave a space between each and finish with a straight section or release the pleats in points as for the peasant blouse on p. 81.

Or you may prefer an important central motif such as the flower basket on p. 23, between upper and lower lines of simple repeated stitchery. The possible combinations are endless.

COLOUR SCHEMES

It is sometimes difficult to decide on the colour outlay for your work. To play safe you should pick not more than three – depending on the background – light, dark and medium colours. White, dark grey, brown, or navy (which is much less harsh than black), may successfully be one of these, while the others may be a paler and a darker shade of one colour.

Do not forget the muted shades of a brighter colour mixed with grey, such as a dusky pink. These are often easier to combine than brighter hues.

Whatever colours you choose the relative amounts in which you use them will help your design. Just a touch of a brighter colour here and there will lift a muted scheme. This is where your sample will be useful.

When deciding, it is much the best plan to take your material along to the shop and lay the colours on it in the proportions you intend to use them: for instance three skeins of light yellow-green, two of deep violet and one of white, on mauve material. By means of trial and error you can in this way arrive at a satisfactory colour scheme.

PREPARING THE PATTERNS

Some of the garment patterns throughout the book are drawn on squared grids. Each square represents 5 cm (2 in) either way. It is possible to buy dressmaking paper already printed with this size of square, each being subdivided for more help. Alternatively, you may prepare your own paper by ruling large sheets, such as wrapping paper.

Copy the lines of the pattern from the diagram. This is easy if you redraw them square by square in the following way: begin at an edge and follow the outline in that one particular square, noting especially where it crosses the grid. Do the same in the subsequent square and so on. Do not forget to copy any lines or marks to help in making up.

When cutting out patterns which do not need a paper template follow either centimetre or inch measurements and do not mix them. It is only possible to change one to the other approximately.

A FEW DRESSMAKING HINTS

Bias strips

Cut a piece of fabric on the straight grain, first pulling threads as a guide. Fold it diagonally to find the bias and press in the fold. Open it out and mark lines parallel with the pressed line at the required width of the bias strips (see Figure 22a). To join the strips, pin the slanting short ends together as shown in Figure 22b, allowing the corners of each strip to project. Stitch, taking a 6 mm (¼ in) seam. Press the seam open and trim off the projecting corners. If you are making a long strip all the joins must slant in the same direction. Make sure of this by checking that each short end has the same slant as shown in Figure 22b.

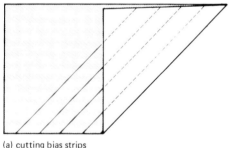

Figure 22A   (a) cutting bias strips

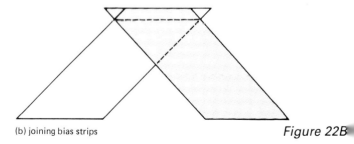

(b) joining bias strips

Figure 22B

Binding

With right sides together, tack and stitch the bias strip to the raw edge taking 6 mm (¼ in) seam allowance. Fold binding over the raw edges to the wrong side of the garment, turn in 6 mm (¼ in) trimming bias if necessary, and slip stitch to first line of stitching.

Rouleaux

A rouleau strip is a neat way of making a cord from fabric, which has many decorative and practical uses including applied surface trimmings and projecting buttonhole loops.

Figure 23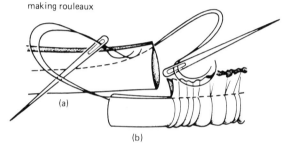

(a)

(b)

Avoid using fabrics which fray easily. Cut a bias strip the length and width required – 2.5 cm (1 in) is enough if you are using fine jersey. Fold lengthwise with the right sides facing. Tack and machine stitch taking a 6 mm (¼ in) seam and leaving top and bottom threads cut at about 25 cm (10 in) long. Thread these through a darning needle and knot them securely. Insert the eye of the needle back into the tube (see Figure 23a) and carefully push and pull the needle back to the other end so that the tube is turned inside out. The finished rouleau may need to be rolled between your fingers so that the seam runs along one side.

You may need to experiment a little before cutting the bias strips to find the correct width, if you are using materials other than jersey. The finished tube will need sufficient seam allowance to fill it: the heavier the fabric, the narrower the seam allowance, and vice versa.

Herring bone stitch

This stitch, which is worked from left to right, makes a useful casing for elastic in addition to its other possibilities. It is

Figure 24   herringbone stitch

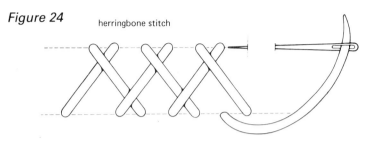

referred to several times in the instructions for making garments. Use one or two thicknesses of thread, and catch up a few threads only on the backs of the smocking pleats. See Figures 24 and 71.

Tailor's tacks

These are useful for marking assembly points on fabric, or for outlining darts. With double threads take two or three stitches through the paper pattern and two layers of fabric. Cut the thread as shown in Figure 25a and remove the pattern. Separate the layers of fabric carefully and snip the lengths of thread pulled

making tailor's tacks

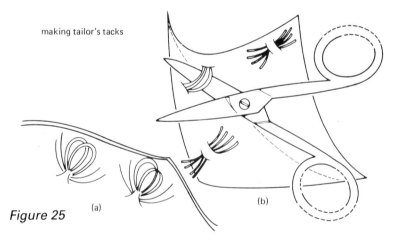

(a)   (b)

Figure 25

in between them, as in Figure 25b. Tailor's tacks may also mark one layer of fabric only. It is a good idea to make the tacks in the same thread you are going to use for the final sewing, as they can sometimes be difficult to remove from machine stitching when you have sewn over them. If a little of the same colour remains trapped it will not be noticed.

Darts

When sewing darts always stitch from the wide end towards the pointed end. Taper this to nothing and cut the threads, leaving approximately 12 mm (½ in) hanging, to prevent the dart becoming unstitched.

Twisted cord

Cut several strands of thread equal to three times the desired length of the finished cord. Fold the strands in half and knot all the ends together, to make a large loop. Slip the knotted end over a doorknob or hook and pull out the threads to the maximum length. Insert a pencil into the loop at the end opposite to the fixed point and turn it in one direction to twist the strands tightly. Fold them in half and allow the cord to twist back on itself. Pull it out with your fingers until the whole length is twisted regularly. If the cord is not firm enough pull it out straight again and twist it a bit more. Knot all the ends together and cut in a tassel. Knot the other end in the same way.

Figure 26

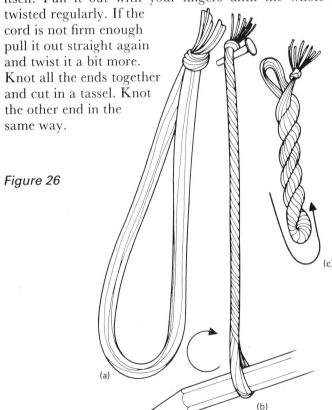

Centimetres and inches

When following instructions use either the number of centi-metres or inches stated, but do not mix the two. All the calculations for these designs have been made in centimetres and it is best to stick to these only. Exact conversion of centimetres to inches requires fractions of an inch which are too small to be practical.

Important: In most cases 1 centimetre is expressed as ⅜ inch – in fact it is slightly larger. However it is important to be exact when marking out or choosing smocking transfers where the measurement between dots and/or rows is given as 8 mm or ⅜ in. Deviation to 1 centimetre will result in the work becoming too big.

4

CHILDREN'S PATTERNS

BABY'S ANGEL TOP

Materials

90 × 80 cm (36 × 31½ in) fine cotton material
Stranded embroidery thread skeins, one each in main colour,
light and medium pinks for the rosettes and green for the leaves
5 small buttons
2 small press studs
2 smocking transfers 26 × 5 cm (10½ × 2 in) for the sleeves and
2 transfers 40 × 5 cm (15¾ × 2 in) for back and front, with dots
and rows 6 mm (¼ in) apart. There should be 8 rows of dots on
each transfer. The number of dots is adjusted when the top is
seamed before smocking
The original is in white with pale blue trellises, pink and green
embroidery

Measurements

To fit chest 45 cm (18 in) – birth to 6 months.

Cutting out

Place all patterns to fold and cut front and back in one piece for
the present. Cut two sleeves. Cut two strips on the straight of
material each 4 × 25 cm (1½ × 10 in) for centre back edgings.

Smocking preparation

The smocking runs all round the neck edges. Apply the transfers
to wrong sides of back, front and sleeves, having top row on each
piece just below raw edge. Cut back vertically up centre. Trim

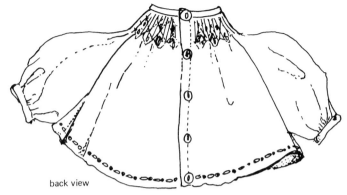

back view

Figure 27

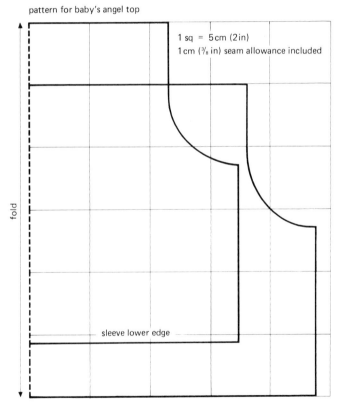

pattern for baby's angel top

1 sq = 5 cm (2 in)
1 cm (3/8 in) seam allowance included

fold

sleeve lower edge

Figure 28

raw edges at armholes a little if necessary so that seam lines will run vertically through a row of dots (see p. 18). With right sides together tack pieces together at armhole, matching smocking dots carefully. Machine stitch, then trim seams to 6 mm (¼ in) and oversew. Starting and finishing rows within approx 1 cm (⅜ in) of centre back edges, gather and draw up threads to 25 cm (10 in).

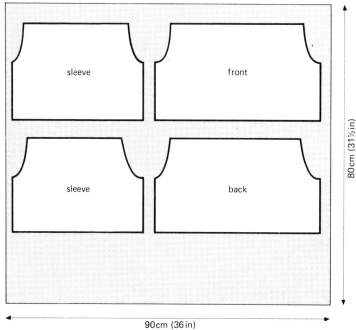

90cm (36in)

80cm (31½in)

Figure 29

Embroidery

The first gathering row is to help in making up and is not included in the stitch diagram. Count the total number of pleats and mark the centre with a pin. Using four strands of the main colour in the needle begin the embroidery to the right of the centre and work outwards to the centre back edge, then turn the work upside down and continue the pattern to the other centre back edge. This will ensure that the patterns on both sides of the centre back stop at the same point. Once this is set you can start at the beginning of each row. Repeat these rows twice more, to

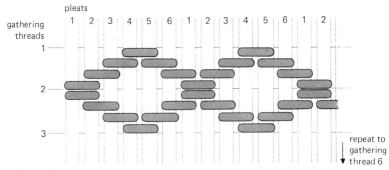

Figure 30

gathering thread 6, then work the seventh row in points by omitting every other repeat. Finish off the thread at the back between points to retain elasticity.

Rosettes Work three rows of rosettes having one rosette in each point on bottom row and placing others following Figure 31. In each diamond take four loose stitches closely spaced over the centre two pleats in pale pink, then space four deep pink stitches around as seen in b, c, d and e of Figure 31. Finish with green 'leaves' as shown in Figure 31f.

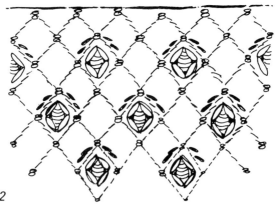

Figure 32

To make up
Withdraw gathering threads.

Centre backs To finish centre backs place raw edge of one 4 cm (1½ in) wide strip next to raw edge of left back, with right sides

Figure 31

together. Seam within 1 cm (⅜ in) of edges, press seam open and fold strip over to inside to enclose raw edge. Press under raw edge of strip and hem to seam line, Figure 33. Neaten raw edges of centre back. On outside sew four buttons evenly spaced down

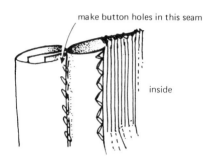

make button holes in this seam

inside

Figure 33

seam line of left centre back, with the top button level with last row of smocking. Finish the right centre back in the same way, but when sewing strip to centre back leave spaces in the seam corresponding to buttons so that when the seam is turned button holes will form.

Side and sleeve seams   With right sides together join side and sleeve seams, trim to 6 mm (¼ in) and neaten.

To complete   Gather sleeve edges to 14 cm (5½ in) or to fit child. Bind with 3 cm (1¼ in) bias strip. Bind neck the same way, extending binding across centre back edges. Press up hem and tack. To decorate and hold hem in place work french knots in main colour at 8 mm (⅜ in) intervals, with detached chain stitches in pale pink in between each. Remove tackings. Sew press studs to hold remainder of centre back in place. At neck edge on right side of centre back opening sew the fifth button to be in line with the other four when fastened.

BABY'S DRESS AND BONNET

Although this dress is sized for a one-year-old it is so loose it will fit for a long time, so make a deep hem to let down. Smocking runs all round the neck edge and round the brim of the bonnet, which is fastened by three buttons down the centre back.

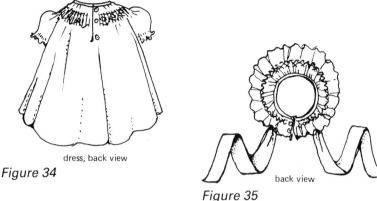

dress, back view

Figure 34

Figure 35

back view

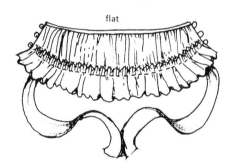

flat

Figure 36

Materials

170 × 114 cm (1¾ yd × 45 in) nylon

Stranded embroidery skeins, 2 light, 1 medium, 1 dark

7 small buttons

3 small press studs

Shirring elastic to match dress

1 m (1 yd) narrow elastic

2 smocking transfers 26 × 4.5 cm (10¼ x 1¾ in) for back and front of dress

2 transfers 30 × 4.5 cm (12 × 1¾ in) for sleeves

1 transfer 134 × 4.5 cm (52½ × 1¾ in) for bonnet, with dots and rows 6 mm (¼ in) apart. There should be 7 rows of dots in each transfer. The exact number of dots does not matter. Join transfers on the back with sticky tape to give the required length where necessary

The original uses pink nylon with white, pink and mauve embroidery

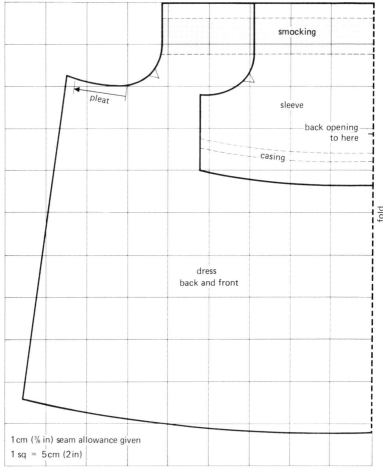

Figure 37

Measurements

To fit chest 51 cm (20 in). Finished length at centre back, 38 cm (15 in), with hem of 10 cm (4 in).

Cutting out

Place all patterns on fold and cut out front and back dress, bonnet, and two bonnet ties each 61 × 6.5 cm (24 × 2½ in). Do not cut centre back opening. Mark position for side pleats, back opening on dress and bonnet ties on bonnet with tailor's tacks.

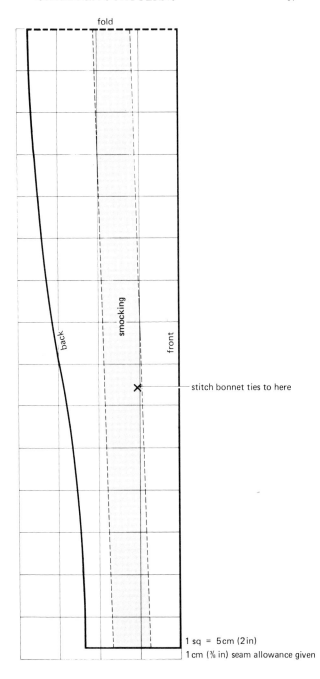

fold

back

smocking

front

X — stitch bonnet ties to here

1 sq = 5 cm (2 in)
1 cm (⅜ in) seam allowance given

Figure 38

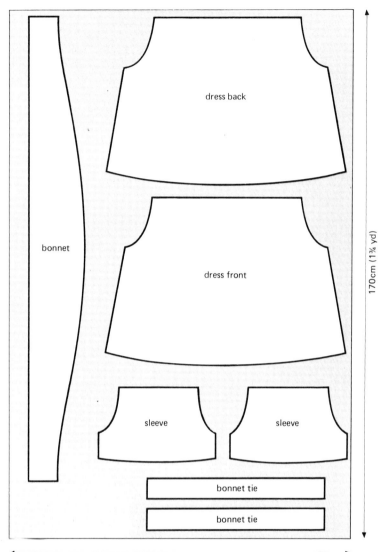

Figure 39

114cm (45in)

170cm (1¾ yd)

Smocking preparation

Turn a very narrow hem to wrong side round sleeves and front
bonnet brim edges. From remainder of material cut two strips on
the cross each 45 × 2.5 cm (17¾ × 1 in). Press in 6 mm (¼ in)

on long edges and sew to wrong side on sleeves as casing for elastic as indicated on pattern. Leave a small gap on one edge to insert elastic. Make soft pleats on dress front and back on outside by folding on solid lines under armholes. Bring folds to seam lines and tack (see Figure 40). Apply the transfers to wrong sides of front, back, sleeves and bonnet as indicated on the pattern. Ensure that a line of dots runs down the centre back.

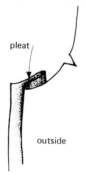

pleat

outside

Figure 40

Dress Tack dress pieces together at armhole edges, first trimming the raw edges if necessary to ensure that the seam will run down a line of dots as described on p. 10. Machine stitch, then trim seams to 6 mm (¼ in) and oversew. Starting and finishing one dot on either side of centre back, gather on smocking dots. Run two gathering threads 1 cm (⅜ in) below raw edge of neck over same area. Draw up all threads to 36 cm (14½ in).

Bonnet Gather on smocking dots. As the bonnet is such a long piece, it may be found easier to gather each row with two lengths of cotton, making the break in each in the same place. Run another two gathering threads 1 cm (⅜ in) below raw edge at the back (unhemmed) edge of the bonnet, for use in making up later. Draw up all threads so that the area to be smocked measures 40 cm (15¾ in). At the break in each row pairs of threads should be tied together (first with second row, etc.) and then cut short, to ensure that surplus will not get in the way of the embroidery.

Embroidery

Using four strands in the needle, work the top three rows of smocking, then use the method as described on p. 20 to centre the rest of the pattern. Finish the design by working three cable stitches in pink as shown under second rope stitch row, then

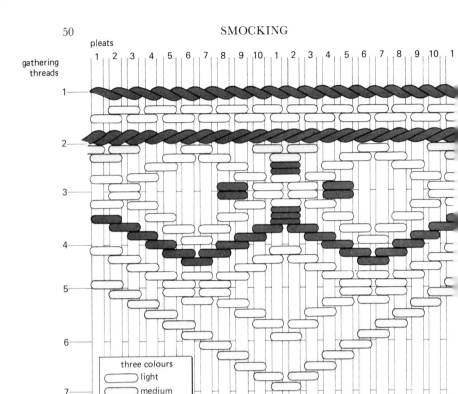

Figure 41

work two or three closely-spaced straight stitches in mauve as shown in the centre of the diagram.

To make up
Withdraw gathering threads.

Dress, back opening Machine stitch along stitching line either side of back opening, as indicated on the pattern, tapering to a point at the bottom. To reinforce the point stitch again over the first stitching. Slash between stitching, see Figure 42. For a continuous lap cut a strip on the straight of the material 38 × 4 cm (15 × 1½ in) and tack right side of strip to wrong side of slash over previous stitching, tapering to nothing at the point. Press under 6 mm (¼ in) on long raw edge of lap and top stitch over seam on outside. Turn right lap to inside and tack in place, see Figure 43.

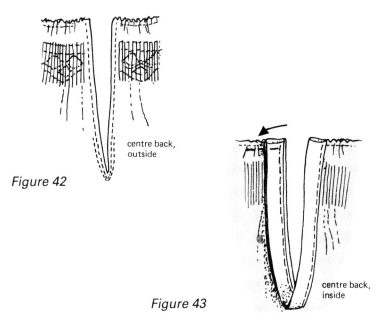

Figure 42

centre back, outside

Figure 43

centre back, inside

Neck edge Trim away material at neck edge just above rows of gathering stitches and bind with 4 cm (1½ in) wide crossway strip, finishing ends of binding parallel with back opening.

To complete dress Stitch entire underarm seam, being careful not to catch in folds of pleats. Insert elastic into sleeve casings and close gaps. Turn up hem. Lap right back over left and sew on three small press studs, top one at neck edge and lowest on a level with gathering thread 6. Sew four buttons at regular intervals on top of right lap.

Bonnet Draw up gathers on back edge to 26 cm (10¼ in) and bind gathered back edge with 4 cm (1½ in) wide crossway strip. Bind straight edges of centre back the same. With shirring elastic make three loops to fit buttons on left centre back, starting at back edge and finishing on a level with the top row of smocking. Sew on buttons to correspond. Narrowly hem long edges and one short edge of strips for tie ends. Gather 1 cm (⅜ in) from raw edges. Pull up gathers tightly, sew ends to marked places inside bonnet.

LITTLE GIRL'S DRESS WITH STRAIGHT YOKE
IN TWO SIZES

Fine cotton/polyester material with a tiny printed spot is used for
this little girl's dress. The spots, 6 mm (¼ in) apart, are used as a
guide for the gathering threads. Narrow stripes will help in the
same way. Alternatively, you may transfer the smocking dots
onto plain material. Pockets are optional. Measurements of the
smaller size are given first. Where only one measurement is given
it applies to both sizes.

Materials

100 × 114 cm (1⅛ yd × 45 in) / 110 × 114 cm (1¼ yd × 45 in)
fine fabric
20 × 114 or 91 cm (8 × 45 or 36 in) for collar in contrasting
fabric
1 smocking transfer 69 × 7 cm / 72 × 7 cm (27 × 2¾ in / 28½ ×
2¾ in) for dress front and 2 transfers 23 × 6 cm (9 × 2¼ in) for

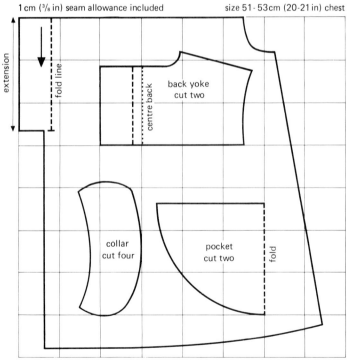

Figure 45

pockets, with dots and rows 6 cm (¼ in) apart. There should be 10 rows of dots on the transfer for the dress front and 8 rows on the transfers for the pockets, including an extra row at the top only for each. The exact number of dots on each row does not matter

The original uses pale blue with white collar, spots and embroidery

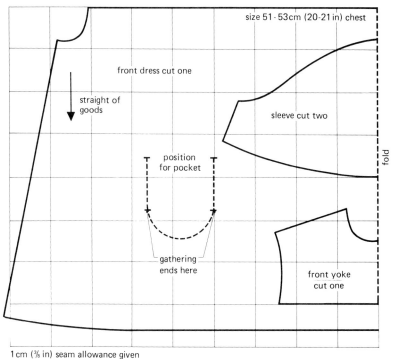

1cm (⅜ in) seam allowance given

Figure 46

Measurements

To fit chest 51–53 cm/53–55 cm (20–21 in/21–22 in); back length 41/45 cm (16¼/17¾ in). 1 year to 18 months/18 months to 2 years.

Cutting out

Figures 45–6 give the pattern in the smaller size. A seam allowance of 1 cm (⅜ in) and a hem of 4 cm (1½ in) have been given.

To make the pattern to the larger size refer to Figure 48. Add 1 cm (⅜ in) on either side to the straight edge A-B on dress front. Add 1 cm (⅜ in) to each dress back along the corresponding edges. Enlarge armholes and side by the same amount as shown. On the yoke front and backs extend shoulder seams C-D by 6 mm (¼ in) and lower straight bottom edges E-F by 6 mm (¼ in), drawing in new armhole lines to meet the ends of these. Enlarge sleeve G-H by 6 mm (¼ in) either side, and lower bottom edge I-J by 1 cm (⅜ in), drawing in a new side edge also.

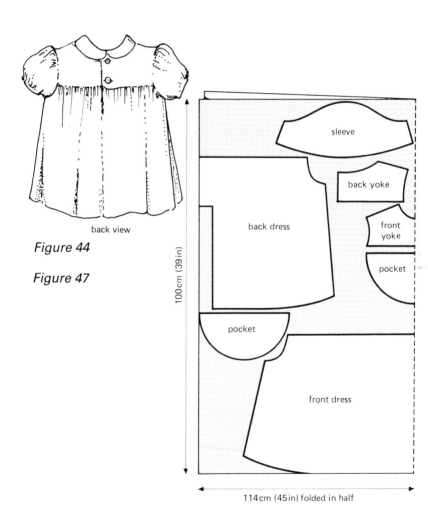

back view

Figure 44

Figure 47

sleeve

back yoke

back dress

front yoke

pocket

pocket

front dress

100cm (39in)

114cm (45in) folded in half

If using spotted material, make sure you lay the upper edge of dress front, backs and pockets along a line of spots. Fold material lengthwise and cut as shown in cutting layout (Figure 47). Cut four collars from contrasting fabric folded lengthwise (not shown). Transfer all markings.

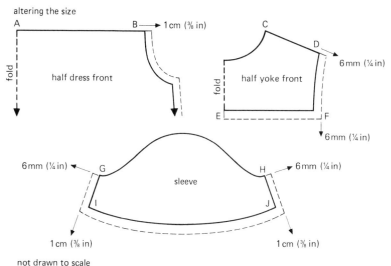

Figure 48

Smocking preparation

If using transfer apply it to the wrong side of dress front, with top row 3 mm (⅛ in) below raw edge, and leaving a margin of 1 cm (⅜ in) blank for seam allowance at either side of the fabric. Turn a very narrow hem to wrong side on straight edge of the pockets.

Apply transfers to wrong sides of pockets with top rows 6 mm (¼ in) below hem, and margins of 1 cm (⅜ in) at either end. If the fabric is semi-transparent do not apply a row of dots to help in making up below lowest row of gathering threads shown on smocking diagrams in case they show on the right side.

If the fabric is spotted gather by picking up the spots so that eleven rows are worked each 6 mm (¼ in) apart. Place top rows as for transferred material. To gather on stripes, first rule pencilled lines 6 mm (¼ in) apart. You may rule and gather an eleventh line if it will not show through the fabric. Leave 1 cm (⅜ in) margin as before. Draw up threads on dress front to 23/24 cm (9/9½ in) and on pockets to 7.5 cm (3 in).

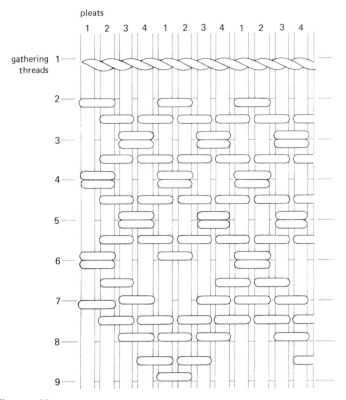

Figure 49

Embroidery

Figure 49 shows the embroidery worked throughout in one colour. The top gathering thread is not shown in the diagram.

Front Work the rope stitch along gathering thread 1. To centre the design correctly on the following trellis row between gathering threads 2 and 3, count to the middle pleat and begin the design here, work to the right edge, turn the work upside down and embroider from the centre to the other edge.

Work the other rows as the pattern is now set. Smock these tiny trellis rows in this way: come up on the left of the first pleat on gathering thread 2 and* take a stitch in pleat 2 with thread above the needle. Take another stitch in pleat 3 halfway between gathering threads 2 and 3, with the thread still above the needle.

Changing position of thread to lie below the needle, stitch into pleat 4 and then up into next pleat halfway between gathering threads 2 and 3 with thread still below the needle. Repeat from*. Diamond stitch can be substituted for this and the following three rows.

Pockets The pocket embroidery is made 12 mm (½ in) shallower by working two trellis rows only.

To make up
Withdraw all gathering threads except the top ones. Take 1 cm (⅜ in) seam throughout.

Collar With right sides together pin and tack outer curved edges together. Machine stitch. Trim seam to 6 mm (¼ in), snip into curves. Turn to right side and press. Catch turned edges together 1 cm (⅜ in) from raw edge for centre front, leave outer ends free.

Yoke Join shoulder seams of front and back yokes. On centre back edges of back yoke press in 6 mm (¼ in) to wrong side and stitch to neaten. With right side facing, pin and tack collars to neck edge, placing join of collars at centre front of yoke, and having raw edges of collars and yoke together. Fold centre back edges to right side 3 cm (1¼ in) away from neatened edge. Tack upper raw edges to neck edge (see Figure 50). From remainder of

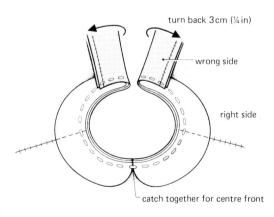

Figure 50

fabric cut sufficient bias strip 2.5 cm (1 in) wide to fit round neck edge. With right sides and raw edges together, pin and tack bias over seam line, starting and finishing within neatened edge of folded back openings. Stitch seam and trim, taking graduated widths from the layers to avoid excessive bulk. Snip into curves. Press bias to inside. Turn yoke backs to inside along fold lines to form facings. Turn under 6 mm (¼ in) on raw edge of bias and slip stitch to inside (see Figure 51).

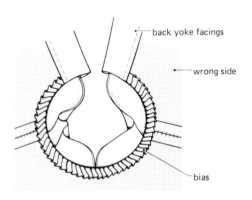

Figure 51

Front dress seam   With right sides together, pin raw edge of yoke front to upper edge of smocking. Back stitch along seam line, catching top of pleats to avoid flattening them. Overcast raw edges together and press seam up.

Back   Press 6 mm (¼ in) to wrong side on long edge of extension on top of centre back seam. Run two gathering threads along top edges of back dress halves, top one 3 mm (⅛ in) away from the edge and the lower one 1 cm (⅜ in) away from fold line to seam allowance. Open out the centre back facings and pin dress backs to back yokes, drawing up gathers to fit. Stitch and press seams up. Press extensions on centre seam to wrong side so that centre folds are in line with back yoke facings. Catch to yoke seams on inside (see Figure 52). Stitch centre back seam on dress, opening out facings and extending seam for 2.5 cm (1 in) inside facings (see Figure 53).

Sleeves   Run two gathering threads along upper edge of sleeves as for dress backs for 9 cm (3¾ in) either side of centre of

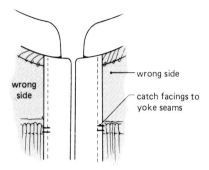

Figure 52

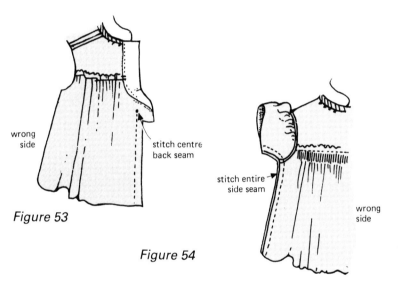

Figure 53

Figure 54

armhole seam. With right sides together pin sleeve to armhole, matching centre to shoulder seams. Draw up gathers to fit. Tack seam and stitch. Stitch again 3 mm (⅛ in) from raw edge. Trim seam close to stitching. Stitch entire side seam, matching armhole seams (see Figure 54). Press 1.5 cm (⅝ in) hem to inside on lower edge of sleeves. Stitch, leaving small opening. Insert elastic to fit through hem.

Pockets   Run gathering threads along seam lines of lower edge of pockets for 7.5 cm (3 in) either side of centre fold line. Draw up gathers to measure 6.5 cm (2½ in). Fold seam allowance to wrong side. Tack pockets to dress as indicated on pattern. Top stitch to dress.

Hem   Decide on length and press fold of hem. Tack close to fold. Run a gathering thread 3 mm (⅛ in) away from raw edge. Pull up gathering so that hem will lie flat and overcast raw edge to neaten. Slip stitch in place.

Back fastening   At centre back lap right facing over left and mark positions for two button holes, having top one 1 cm (⅜ in) away from top edge and lower one 1 cm (⅜ in) away from yoke seam. The ends of the button holes should be placed 1 cm (⅜ in) away from folded edge. Sew on buttons to correspond.

LITTLE GIRL'S PINAFORE DRESS

The smocking on this pinafore is quick and very effective in thick soft embroidery cotton. Front and back are embroidered. Smocking pleats are deep so that you may use fine wool. The skirt can be made without the contrast band and be trimmed with patterned ribbon instead of ric-rac braid.

Figure 55

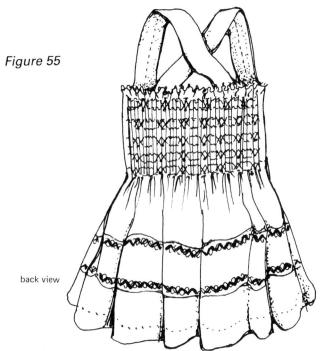

back view

Materials

Contrast version:
100 × 91 cm (1¼ yds × 36 in) fine wool
20 × 91 cm (¼ yd × 36 in) contrasting fabric
4 m (4½ yds) ric-rac braid

Self-coloured version:
Same amount of fine wool
2 m (2¼ yd) ric-rac

For both:
Soft embroidery thread skeins, 1 light, 4 medium, 1 dark
Chenille needle for embroidery
2 m (2¼ yds) narrow seam binding to match main colour of material
2 smocking transfers each 13 × 82.5 cm (5 × 32½ in) with dots 8 mm (⅜ in) and rows 12 mm (½ in) apart (see p. 10). There should be 11 rows of 87 dots on each, including an extra row at the bottom only
The original, in bright Tyrolean colours, uses fine scarlet flannel wool with white, gold and emerald green embroidery, emerald contrast and white ric-rac braid

Measurements

To fit chest 61 cm (24 in), length 38 cm (15 in), with 6.5 cm (2½ in) hem allowed. The seam allowance is 1 cm (⅜ in). To vary the size, slight alterations are needed. The bodice smocking allows for chest expansion up to 5 cm (2 in) larger, but you may alter the skirt and strap length. To make the pinafore smaller, take 6 mm (¼ in) more seam width at either side for every 2.5 cm (1 in) smaller than the given size.

Cutting out

Contrast version: fold main colour fabric in half across the width and cut two pieces each 24 × 88 cm (9½ × 34½ in) and two pieces each 15 × 88 cm (6 × 34½ in). Cut two pieces contrasting fabric 10 × 88 cm (4 × 34½ in) – not shown in cutting layout. Self-coloured version: fold fabric as for contrast version and cut two pieces 45 × 88 cm (18 × 34½ in). For both versions cut 2 straps 45 × 10 cm (17¾ × 4 in).

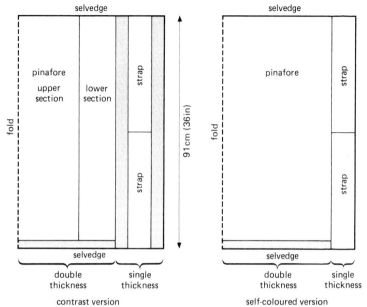

Figure 56

selvedge

Smocking preparation, both versions

Take the two largest pieces of the main-colour fabric and press in 1 cm (⅜ in) to the wrong side along one long edge of each. Open out the fold. Tack ric-rac as shown in Figure 57, then tack seam binding over half the width of the ric-rac and the raw edge of the material. Stitch seam binding edge in the centre of the ric-rac.

Figure 57

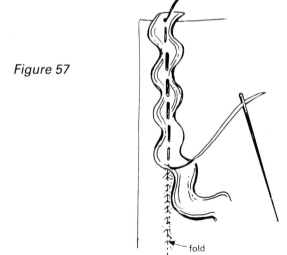

Refold where pressed and hem lower edge of seam binding to wrong side (see Figure 58). Apply the transfers to the wrong sides of front and back pieces so that the top row of dots runs just below the hemmed edge of the seam binding, with approximately 3.5 cm (1¼ in) on either side. Gather and draw up threads to measure 26 cm (10¼ in).

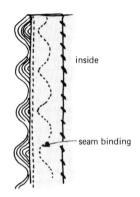

Figure 58

Embroidery

Following the stitch diagram begin on gathering thread 1 with light colour. Work five cable stitches, then go down to thread 2 to begin diamond stitch in pleat 7. With thread below the needle take pleats 7 and 8 together. Go up to gathering thread 1 with thread still below the needle to the next pleat and repeat the pattern along the row ten times. Work the five cable stitches of

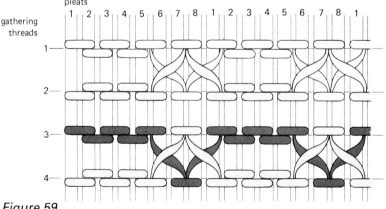

Figure 59

the next repeat and finish off. Begin the next row, which crosses over the previous one, on gathering thread 2 in medium colour. These two rows are repeated five times in all, using a combination of light and medium colours for the first and alternate repeats and medium and dark colours for the second and fourth repeats. The last gathering thread is for help in embroidering the last repeat only.

To make up
Withdraw gathering threads and join side seams. Press seams open and overcast to neaten.

Ric-rac embroidery, contrast version   Ric-rac is couched all round at the top and bottom of the contrast strip. Tack ric-rac in place overlapping ends and matching curves. With medium-colour thread double in the needle and following Figure 60 come up at A, down at B, up at C, down at D and so on. Work the return journey in the same colour, as shown in Figure 60.

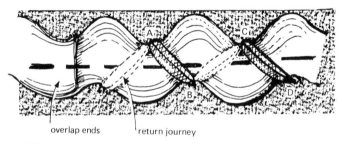

overlap ends   return journey

Figure 60

Straps   With right sides together fold straps in half lengthways and sew long edges together. Press seams open and turn to inside, press again so that seams run down the centre of one side. Oversew the ends to the inside of the pinafore intended for the front, adjusting length if necessary, and sew press studs to the other ends so that straps may be crossed over and fastened inside the back. Turn up hem. Extra firmness may be obtained on upper and lower smocking edges by working herring bone stitch over elastic on inside, as described on pp. 35–6.

CHILD'S DRESS WITH SMOCKED BODICE

The rich smocking on this bodice completely covers the whole of the front, making the chest very elastic and comfortable to wear. With a deep hem to let down it will be party wear for a long time, justifying the amount of work lavished on it. What better way to show off your skill in needlework?

Figure 61

Figure 62

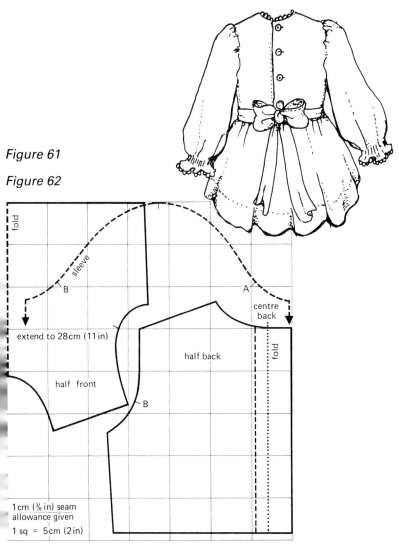

Materials

160 × 114 cm (1¾ yd × 45 in) material
Stranded embroidery thread skeins, 2 light, 1 medium, 1 dark
110 cm (43 in) narrow trimming
4 small buttons
66 cm (26 in) bias binding to match dress
Smocking transfer 100 × 28 cm (39 × 11 in) with dots and rows
6 mm (¼ in) apart. There should be 45 rows of dots down the
depth of 28 cm (11 in), including an extra one at the top and
bottom. The exact number of dots across the rows does not
matter. Join transfers on the back with sticky tape to give the
required measurements
The original uses mid-blue Viyella with white, raspberry pink
and deep hyacinth-blue embroidery, and white trimming

Measurements

To fit chest 61–66 cm (24–26 in), length 57 cm (22½ in) with 5
cm (2 in) hem allowed; sleeve seam, adjustable, 28 cm (11 in).

Figure 63

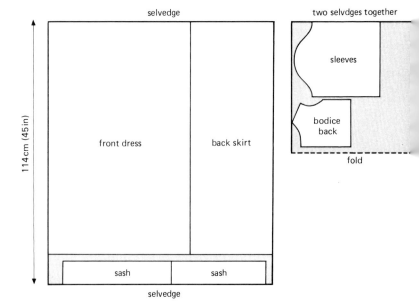

Cutting out

Seam allowance of 1 cm (⅜ in) has been given. Cut two bodice backs and two sleeves, reversing pattern if necessary, two sashes 48 × 10 cm (19 × 4 in); one back skirt 102 × 38 cm (40 × 15 in), one front dress 102 × 65 cm (40 × 25½ in). Transfer all markings. From stiff paper only cut one complete bodice front.

Smocking preparation

The smocking is on the front bodice only, which is then cut out after the embroidery has been worked. Apply the transfer to the wrong side of one end of the front dress piece. Make sure this is straight by first pulling a thread. The top row of the transfer should run 6 mm (¼ in) below the raw edge and there should be a margin of 1 cm (⅜ in) at either end. Gather and draw up threads to measure 33 cm (13 in) across. Find centre pleat and mark with a contrast thread. Fold pattern for bodice front in half lengthways and pin bottom layer to material with right side facing so that fold runs down the centre pleat and upper shoulder edge is level with top raw edge of material. See Figure 64.

Figure 64

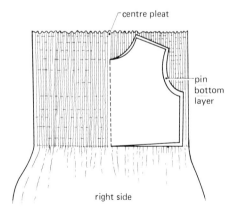

Without removing pins, unfold the paper and pin the other half in place. Tack round the outline of neck, shoulders and armholes with contrasting thread – Figure 65.

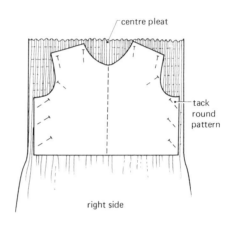

Figure 65

Embroidery

To save time and thread, work the smocking to start and finish not less than 2 cm (¾ in) outside the lines of tacking. Use four strands in the needle. Follow the stitch diagram (Figure 66), and remember that the top and bottom thread are to help in making up only and are omitted in it. Begin on gathering thread 1 with the light colour and work two rows of paired diamond stitch to thread 3. Start the next row immediately below thread 3 to give a continuous pattern, and repeat these rows to thread 11. The smocking at this point should equal the depth of the neck. Begin the main pattern with a row in stem stitch in medium colour on thread 12 and a paired row in dark colour just above it. These two rows should run from armhole to armhole.

To avoid mistakes in centring the design begin the next row of trellis stitch by coming up on the left of the marked centre pleat ready to take the stitch indicated by A on Figure 66. Continue to the right-hand edge, then turn the work upside down and come

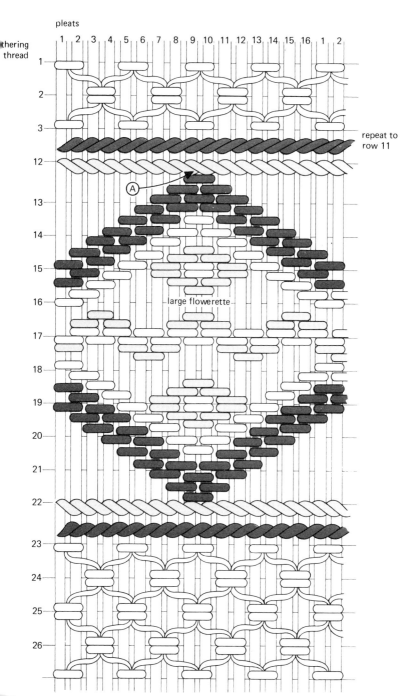

Figure 66

up in the starting place on the centre pleat. Work to the other edge. Now the pattern has been set, all the subsequent rows can be started in the usual way at the left-hand edge. The large flowerettes on gathering thread 15 are described on p. 30. The total depth of the pattern can be changed by altering the number of rows of paired diamond stitch over threads 23 to 27. After working these two paired diamond stitch rows repeat rows 12 to 26 once more, then make a pointed edge by working alternate diamond stitches only on the last row.

To make up

Withdraw gathering threads and compare finished shape of smocking with paper pattern. If it has altered, retack the outline carefully, centring the pattern as before. Run two lines of machine stitching just inside the tacked line then remove the tacking.

Back Turn 6 mm (¼ in) hem along back bodices, press in centre back edges to wrong side along fold lines to form facings.

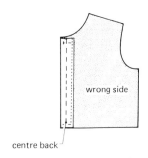

centre back

Figure 67

Tack in place horizontally at top and bottom, see Figure 67. Overlap right back bodice over left, matching centre back lines, Figure 68. Tack in place at lower edge. Gather skirt back and sew to bodice backs at waist.

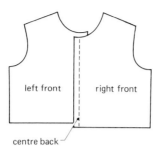

left front | right front

centre back

Figure 68

Sashes   Turn 6 mm (¼ in) hem on long sides of sashes, cut one short end of each in a slant and turn same hem allowance on slanted edges. Fold the other ends in three and tack short folded ends parallel to raw edges of front smocking in line with bottom of bodice (Figure 69).

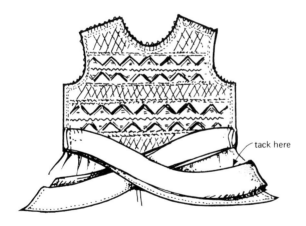

tack here

Figure 69

Shoulder and side seams   With right sides together, tack front to back at shoulder and side edges, enclosing raw ends of sashes. Stitch, press seams open and neaten.

Neck   Cut bias strip 3 cm (1¼ in) wide to fit all round neck plus 3 cm (1¼ in) extra. Turn in 12 mm (½ in) on one short end and with right sides facing pin binding to neck, stretching slightly round curves. Turn in the raw edge on the other short end and snip off any excess. Taking seam allowance of 1 cm (⅜ in) tack and stitch. Cut away seam allowance to 6 mm (¼ in) (see Figure 70). Turn binding to wrong side, fold raw edge to inside and hem down just inside stitching line, closing ends of binding.

Figure 70

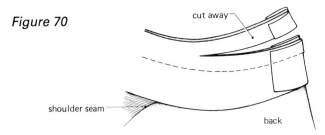

cut away

shoulder seam

back

Sleeves   Sew underarm seam, taking care to have a pair if material is reversible. Press open. Turn a narrow hem round lower edge. Sew bias tape casing 12 mm (½ in) away from lower hemmed edge to inside of sleeve, folding raw ends to the inside so that an opening is left to insert wrist elastic. Gather sleeve tops between balance marks A and B 6 and 12 mm (¼ and ½ in) away from raw edges (see Figure 62). Turn dress inside out and with right sides of dress and sleeves facing match top centre,

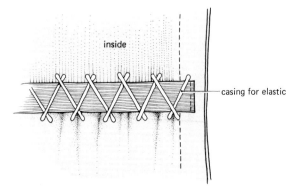

inside

casing for elastic

Figure 71

underarm seams and balance marks, draw up gathers to fit, tack and stitch. Press seam towards sleeve.

Finishing Make four button holes on right side of centre back opening, first one 12 mm (½ in) from top. Sew hook and eye to overlap at neck edge. Catch narrow trimming to inside of neck and sleeve ends and insert wrist elastic. Turn up hem. If necessary catch ends of a length of elastic to side seams of front bodice on inside and hold in place with herring bone stitches, to take the strain of the sash being tied (see p. 36 and Figure 71).

GINGHAM DRESS IN FOUR SIZES

This dress will fall to mid-calf, but it can be made any length and would also be pretty made up as a nightie. Sleeves and frill can pick up the main colour of the gingham or can be cut from the same material. The yoke smocking is not the conventional type as the material is drawn up while you work, and so it does not

Figure 72

back view

need a transfer or gathering threads. It reduces the width of the fabric to just under a half. Surface honeycomb in the same colour throughout is the only stitch used. Its main effect is to repattern the fabric decoratively. The same technique can be used on stripes, but you will need to draw horizontal lines as guides.

Materials

Twice the desired length of the dress in polyester/cotton gingham 114 cm (45 in) wide with 6 mm (¼ in) checks for front and back
40 × 114 cm (½ yd × 45 in) of contrast for sleeves and frill
1 ball Sylko Perlé no 5 or 1 skein stranded cotton
30 cm (12 in) narrow elastic
The original uses brown and white gingham with white embroidery

Measurements

To fit chest 56/61/66/71 cm (22/24/26/28 in) loosely. Instructions are given in this order. If only one figure is given it applies to all.

Cutting out

Seam allowance of 1 cm (⅜ in) has been given. There is no cutting layout diagram. Cut the desired length across the fabric width for front and back. The yoke will be shaped after the material has been smocked. Noting that gingham has a two-row pattern of checks, level off one widthwise edge of each piece along the upper edge of a row containing dark checks for the top yoke edge (see Figure 73). Cut the sleeves and frill from the remainder or from contrast. Cut two frills across the width, each 10 × 99/104/109/114 cm (4 × 39/41/43/45 in). Fold the

Figure 73

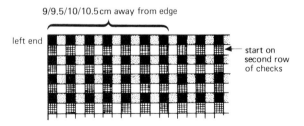

9/9.5/10/10.5 cm away from edge

left end

start on second row of checks

remaining piece in half lengthwise and cut two sleeves each 15/16/18/19 cm × 36/41/46/51 cm (6/6½/7/7½ × 14/16/18/20 in).

Smocking preparation

The smocking runs across the front yoke only. The back yoke may be smocked also or it may be gathered into a bias band. The smocking is gathered as it is worked so that no preparations are needed.

Embroidery

As the dress is all in one piece, allowance must be made on either side of the yoke for the underarm. This means that the first row should be started 9/9.5/10/10.5 cm (3½/3¾/4/4½ in) away from the left-hand edge on the second row of checks as explained in the cutting-out instructions (see Figure 73). All horizontal stitches are drawn up so that the gingham checks are pulled together and all diagonal ones are left flat on the surface. The diagram shows the horizontal stitches before they are pulled up. Rows of checks not worked are left unshaded. Work from left to right.

Row 1 Following the stitch diagram (Figure 74), come up in the top left-hand corner of square A^1 (dark two-tone) and take a tiny stitch of two or three threads only in the top right corner of the same square. Keep all subsequent stitches the same size. Draw up the thread firmly but not overtightly, thus pulling these corners together. Stitch into the bottom right corner of the same square, draw up the thread so that it lies flat on the surface. Stitch through the bottom right corner of square B^1 (white), draw up firmly. Stitch through the top right corner of the same square B^1, leave thread lying flat. Continue along the same line of A^1 and B^1 checks until the embroidery measures 20/21.5/23/24 cm (8/8½/9/9½ in). Finish off. All the dark checks will be drawn together on the row below, which is left unworked.

Row 2 Come up in the *bottom* left corner of square A^2, stitch into bottom right corner of square A^2. Draw up the thread. Stitch into top right corner of A^2; leave thread flat. Continue along the line of checks as for row 1. The upper row of horizontal stitches will be placed directly under the lower line in the row above.

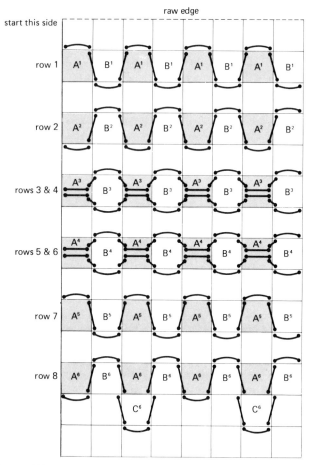

Figure 74

When the embroidery is complete the line of checks underneath will be drawn into honeycomb effect. Do not work on this line.

Row 3 This occupies only half a row of checks in depth. Come up on the left-hand side of A^3 halfway down, take a stitch in the right side of the same square on the same level. Draw up thread. Take a stitch in the top right corner of A^3; leave thread flat. Continue along the row, placing the lower line of stitches halfway down the checks. The upper line lies in between the lower line on the previous row.

Row 4   This pairs up with the previous row. Come up on the left of A^3 touching the lower line on the previous row; stitch into the right side of the same square. Draw up thread. Stitch into bottom right corner of A^3; leave thread flat. Continue along the row. The dark checks only will show on the row below, which should be left unworked.

Rows 5 and 6   Omit these rows for the first two sizes only. For the remaining two work them over checks A^4 and B^4 exactly as for rows 3 and 4. The checks below will be drawn into honeycomb effect.

Row 7   As for row 1, over checks A^5 and B^5.

Row 8   Finish with a row of points. Beginning as for row 2, come up in the bottom left corner of A^6, stitch over to bottom right of the same square, draw up thread. Stitch into top right of A^6; leave thread flat.* Stitch over to top right of B^6; draw up thread. Stitch into bottom right of the same square; leave thread flat, then into bottom left of C^6 (dark) on row immediately below; again leave thread flat. Stitch across to bottom right of the same square; draw up thread. Stitch into top right of the same square; leave thread flat. Then into top right of A^6; again leave thread flat. Take the next 4 stitches over 1 row of checks only as for row 1, then repeat from * along the row, thus forming a point in between every complete honeycomb stitch.

To make up

Yoke   Following Figure 75, trim the smocked yoke to the measurements given, which include 1 cm (⅜ in) seam allowance on all edges. Trim the rest of the piece straight down the sides. If the back is to be left plain cut it according to the width of the front at its lower edge. Cut out the armholes to the same measurements and gather the top so that it corresponds with the front. From remnants cut two strips 4 cm (1½ in) wide to bind the top raw edges.

Side seams   With right sides facing, place back and front together and join side seams within 1 cm (⅜ in) from side edges.

cut only when smocking has been worked
drawn to scale 4:1

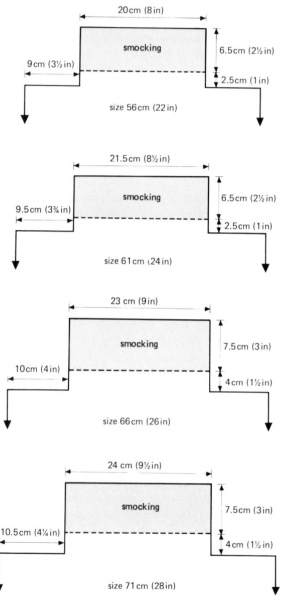

Figure 75

Frill With right sides together, join frill pieces along short edges and turn a narrow hem along one long edge. Run a gathering thread 1 cm (⅜ in) from the other long edge. The easiest way to do this is to loosen upper tension on your sewing machine and set it to its longest stitch, then pull up the bobbin thread. With right sides together place the gathered edge of the frill to the raw edge of the dress and stitch. Trim seam and oversew.

Sleeves Press in a hem of 1 cm (⅜ in) wide to wrong side on one long edge of sleeves and tack. Press in 1 cm (⅜ in) to wrong side along short edges – there is no need to turn a hem here. With right sides of dress and sleeves facing, pin sleeves over yoke and armhole edges 1 cm (⅜ in) away from raw edges of dress. Tack and top stitch close to pressed-in edge all round neck and armhole edges of sleeves. Snip into yoke and armhole edge at right-angled corner on inside (see Figures 76 and 77). With right

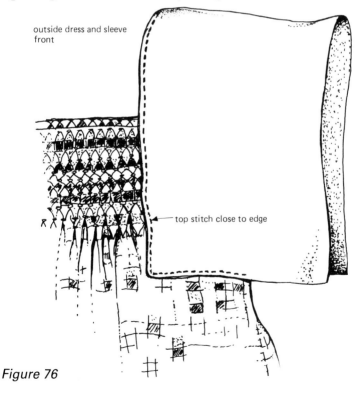

outside dress and sleeve front

top stitch close to edge

Figure 76

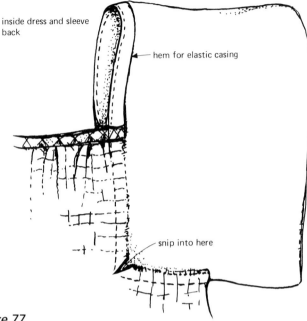

inside dress and sleeve
back

hem for elastic casing

snip into here

Figure 77

sides together join remaining short edges of sleeves 1 cm (⅜ in)
away from edge. Turn a narrow hem to inside along remaining
raw edge of sleeve. Slip stitch along hem at neck edge between
back and front yokes, run through narrow elastic so that sleeves
are gathered to fit and secure ends.

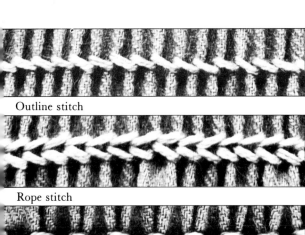

Outline stitch

Rope stitch

Single cable

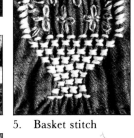

5. Basket stitch

Double cable

Diamond stitch

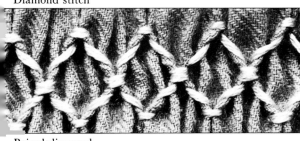

Paired diamond

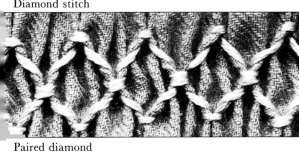

Cross diamond stitch

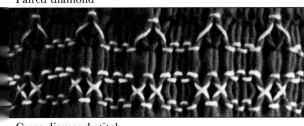

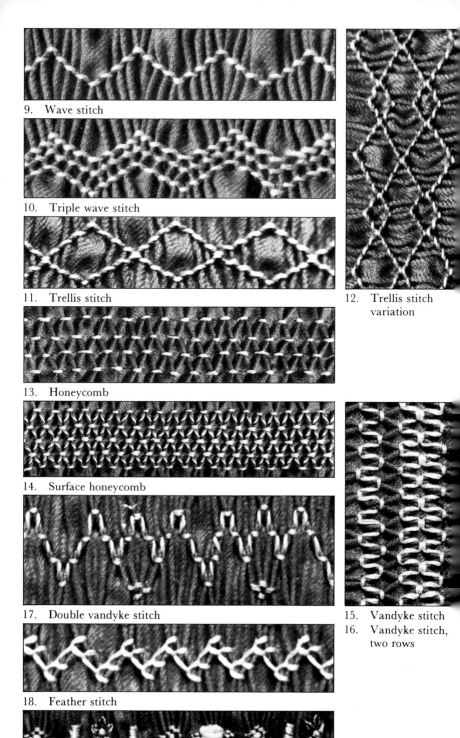

9. Wave stitch

10. Triple wave stitch

11. Trellis stitch

12. Trellis stitch variation

13. Honeycomb

14. Surface honeycomb

17. Double vandyke stitch

15. Vandyke stitch
16. Vandyke stitch, two rows

18. Feather stitch

19. Decorative stitches for isolated use: spool stitch, small and large flowerettes, chain stitch flowerettes, bullion stitch roses

Baby's angel top

Baby's dress and bonnet

Little girl's dress with straight yoke

Little girl's pinafore dress

Gingham dress in four sizes

Girl's dress with smocked bodice

Peasant blouse

Edwardian-style blouse

Gingham smock to go over trousers

Skirt with tapered back and
front panels

Sun dress or nightdress

Sleeveless waistcoat

Smock dress

Gingham sun hat

Square and round cushions in Canadian smocking

Skirt with panels in Canadian smocking

Bag with wooden beads

5
ADULTS' PATTERNS

PEASANT BLOUSE

Nothing could be more simple than this blouse, made from rectangles, with square sleeves with a gusset set in the under arms. In fine wool jersey it becomes a winter overblouse. Cut a little longer it becomes a tunic, perhaps with slits in the side seams, or it may grow into a belted dress. Smocking shapes the neck into a circle which can be altered by a drawstring. The length of the sleeves may be varied, or they may be gathered into the bias bands without being smocked.

Figure 78

back view

Materials

280 × 114 or 91 cm (3 yd × 45 or 36 in) cotton
Sylko Perlé no 5
1 ball each of light, medium, dark, or 3 skeins each stranded
embroidery cotton in the same colours
6 smocking transfers each 66 × 7.5 cm (26 × 3 in) with dots and
rows 6 mm (¼ in) apart. There should be 12 rows of 105 dots on
each transfer, which includes an extra row at the top only
The original uses light apricot cotton with cream, orange and
dark brown embroidery

Measurements

To fit bust 87–97 cm (34–38 in), length at centre back and front
70 cm (27½ in), sleeve seam 36 cm (14 in).

Cutting out

1 cm (⅜ in) seam allowance has been given. Cut back and front
each 68 × 72 cm (26¾ × 28¼ in), two sleeves each 68 × 63.5 cm
(26¾ × 25 in), two gussets each 9 cm (3½ in) square.

Figure 79

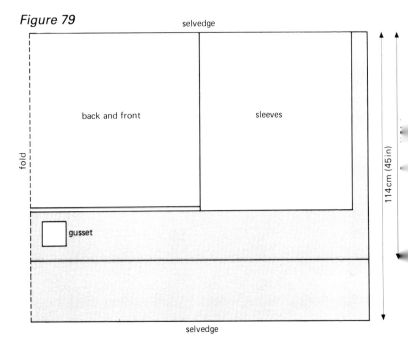

Smocking preparation

Apply the transfers to the longer edge of front and back with top rows 6 mm (¼ in) below raw edge, and to both longer edges of each sleeve, with top row of one transfer and lowest row of the other also 6 mm (¼ in) from raw edge. Following Figure 80, pin and tack the back, front and sleeves together for 25 cm (10 in) from neck edge and tack the sleeve seams for 10 cm (4 in) from wrist edges. Match the dots carefully at row ends so that seams will run through a row of dots. Count the *spaces* between dots; there should be 104 on wrist ends of each sleeve and between each seam round neck. Machine stitch along tackings. Gather and draw up sleeves to 23 cm (9 in), and neck to 80 cm (31½ in). As the neck is such a long piece you may gather each row with two or more lengths of cotton, making the break in each in the same place. For further suggestions see the instructions for smocking preparation on the skirt with shaped back and front panels on p. 101.

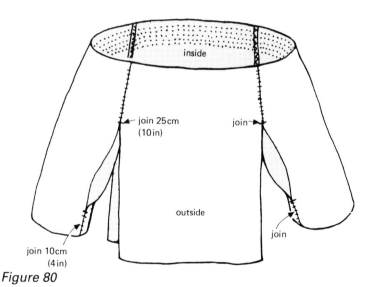

inside

join 25cm
(10in)

join→

outside

join

join 10cm
(4in)

Figure 80

Embroidery

The top row is for help in making up only and is not included in the stitch diagram (Figure 81). Follow the arrangement of stitches as given until you have worked the row of surface

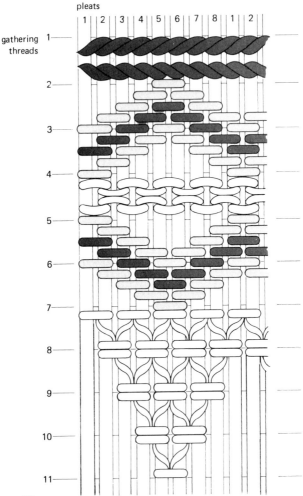

Figure 81

honeycomb between threads 8 and 9, then continue each point
separately in this way: referring to Figure 81, come up in pleat 2
on one of the repeats and work over pleats 2 to 1 on the next
repeat between gathering threads 8 to 9. Turn work upside
down, come up in pleat 8 and work back to pleat 3 between
threads 9 and 10. Finally turn work right side up again, come up
in pleat 4 and work to pleat 7 to finish the point between threads
10 to 11. Finish off.

There should be exactly thirteen repeats of the pattern on the wrist ends of the sleeves and fifty-two repeats round the neck.

To make up

Withdraw all gathering threads except the top one. Insert the gusset following instructions for making up the smock dress on p. 125, then join the remaining sleeve and seam edges. Trim seams back to 6 mm (¼ in) where this has not already been done and overcast. Cut and join enough strips on the bias 4 cm (1½ in) wide to go round neck and sleeve edges. Bind sleeves. Turn in one end of the neck binding for about 1 cm (⅜ in) to give a straight edge and apply it to the neck with right sides together, starting at the centre front edge. End at the same place, trimming the binding to give 1 cm (⅜ in) to turn in at the other straight edge. Do not join the ends. Make a twisted cord, following instructions on p. 37 from eight lengths of Perlé cotton or twelve lengths of stranded cotton, and thread it through the neck binding. Turn a narrow hem at the bottom of the blouse.

EDWARDIAN STYLE BLOUSE

This blouse may be varied by omitting the lace trimming from the front or by making the three-quarter sleeves full length. For these 20 cm (¼ yd) more material should be allowed.

Figure 82

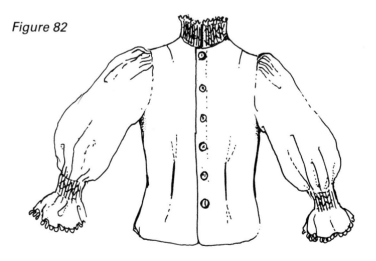

Materials

220 × 114 cm (2½ yd × 45 in) cotton and polyester lawn
Stranded embroidery thread skeins, 1 each in light and medium,
2 in dark
3 m (3¼ yd) narrow lace
80 cm (32 in) cluny (heavy cotton) lace, approximately 4 cm (1½
in) wide
6 buttons
3 small hooks and eyes
40 cm (16 in) narrow soft elastic
Smocking transfer 144 × 6 cm (56¾ × 2½ in) for collar
2 transfers 67 × 7.5 cm (26½ × 3 in) for sleeves, with dots and
rows 6 mm (¼ in) apart. There should be 10 rows of 227 dots on
the collar transfer and 11 rows of 105 dots on each of the sleeve
transfers. These include one extra row at the bottom only. Join
transfers on the back with sticky tape
The original uses cream lawn with white, apricot and light
brown embroidery and cream lace trimming

Measurements

To fit 83/87/92 cm (32/34/36 in) bust loosely; length at centre
back 66 cm (26 in); sleeve seam 42 cm (16½ in) including frill.

Cutting out

No seam allowance has been given on the pattern, so allow 1 cm
(⅜ in) on all edges. The pattern shown is in size 87 cm (34 in).
For a size *smaller* cut off 6 mm (¼ in) at shoulder and 12 mm (½
in) at side back and fronts; adjust length of bust dart to measure
13.5 cm (5¼ in). For a size *larger* add on these amounts at sides
and shoulder; adjust length of bust dart to 13.5 cm (5¼ in). The
sleeve remains the same for all sizes; extend pattern to desired
length. Cut two half backs, two sleeves and one front, folding the
material as indicated on the cutting layout. Cut one collar 148 ×
10 cm (58½ × 4 in), the same measurements for all sizes (not
shown on the pattern). Do not cut out the shoulder darts.
Transfer all markings including the waist pleats. If preferred you
may use an existing blouse bodice pattern and cut the sleeves
and collar as shown in Figures 83 and 84.

Figure 83

size 87 cm (34 in) adjustable

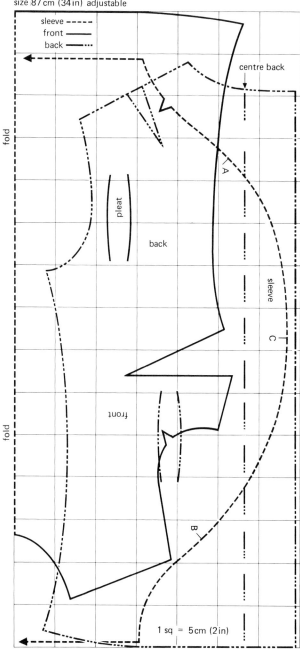

sleeve - - - - -
front ———
back —··—··—

centre back

fold

fold

pleat

back

A

sleeve

C

front

B

1 sq = 5 cm (2 in)

no seam allowance given

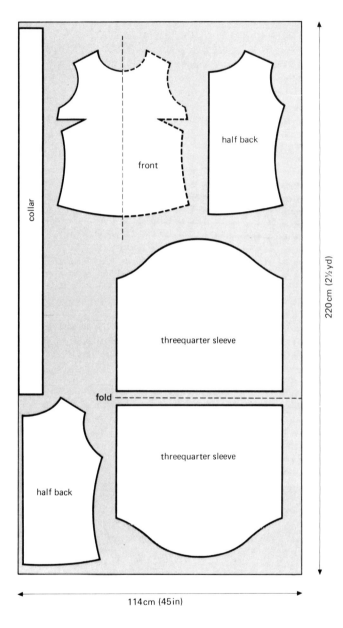

Figure 84

Smocking preparation

Collar   Turn a narrow hem not wider than 6 mm (¼ in) on one long edge of the collar and edge with narrow lace. Apply transfer to wrong side of the collar so that the top row is just below the hem. There should be an undotted area of material 2.5 cm (1 in) wide at either end.

Sleeves   Apply smocking transfers to wrong sides of sleeves with lowest row 5 cm (2 in) above lower edge. Make sure you have a pair of sleeves. Turn a hem not wider than 6 mm (¼ in) on lower edge and trim as for collar. Place transfer within seam allowance at either side. Taking a seam allowance of 1 cm (⅜ in) throughout the garment, pin and tack the sleeve seams for 15 cm (6 in) only from lower edge. Match the rows of smocking dots and make sure the seam runs through a vertical line of dots to ensure that the gathering threads will be circular, as explained on p. 10. Turn a narrow hem on lower edge and trim with lace to match collar.

Gathering   Gather and draw up threads to 33 cm (13 in) on collar and 19 cm (7½ in) on sleeves. Check that there are 226 pleats on collar and 104 pleats on right side of each sleeve.

Embroidery

Collar   Work as shown on the smocking diagram with four strands in the needle. Repeat the central diamond-shaped pattern twenty-eight times along the row. Finish by taking two stitches in the centre, as shown, on gathering thread 5, carrying the stranded cotton loosely at the back of the work from one group to the other.

Sleeves   Enlarge the design slightly by working down to gathering thread 5, then make a line of cable stitches instead of the groups of 2 in light thread along the row. Follow the diagram to finish.

To make up

Withdraw gathering threads.

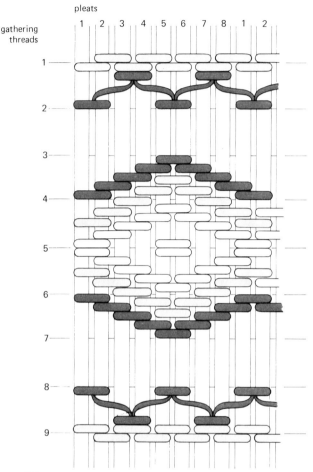

Figure 85

Bodice Join darts on front, press upwards. Dart shoulders on backs, press towards armholes. Join shoulder and side seams. Turn a narrow hem to wrong side on centre back edge and on lower edge. Stitch two pleats on front and one on each half back on inside at waistline by joining lines shown on pattern.

Collar Turn the unworked 2.5 cm (1 in) at each end to the inside, trim away 1 cm (⅜ in) and take a 1 cm (⅜ in) hem. Trim along lower edge to 1 cm (⅜ in) below last line of smocking. With right sides facing, tack raw edges of collar and neck edges together starting and finishing at centre back markings on back bodices. The collar should be attached to the bodice just below the last line of smocking. Machine stitch, then trim away the seam allowance 6 mm (¼ in) below stitching and overcast to neaten. Sew three small hooks to right end of collar and eyes to correspond on left end. To ensure that the top of the collar will fit close to the neck, pin narrow soft elastic or three strands of shirring elastic close to the upper edge on the inside and work herring bone stitch over the elastic (see p. 36).

Centre back opening   Turn 1 cm (⅜ in) to inside at the top edge of centre backs (see Figure 86). Fold each hemmed edge to inside so that there is an extension of 2 cm (¾ in) beyond each end of the collar and the raw edge is enclosed. Slip stitch over lower neatened edge of collar (Figure 87). Make six button holes on right centre back, having the left end of each 1 cm (⅜ in) away from folded edge. The top one should be 1 cm (⅜ in) down from collar seam and remainder at 10-cm (4-in) intervals.

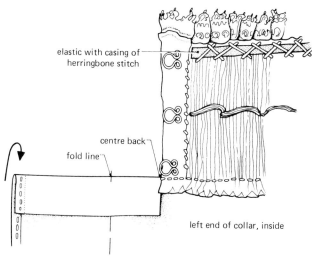

elastic with casing of
herringbone stitch

centre back

fold line

left end of collar, inside

Figure 86

Sleeves   Join rest of sleeve seam. Gather sleeve tops between marked points, A and B (see Figure 83) 3 mm and 6 mm (⅛ and ¼ in) away from raw edges. With right sides together, pin

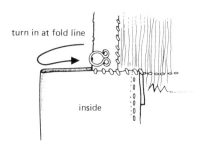

Figure 87

sleeves into armholes matching top centre C to shoulder seam, underarm to side seam of bodice, and front balance mark. Draw up gathering thread to fit armhole. Tack on seam line and machine stitch. Trim seam to 6 mm (¼ in) and oversew.

To finish   Gather wide lace and sew to front in a curve between shoulder seams.

GINGHAM SMOCK TO GO OVER TROUSERS

This smock is designed to go over trousers or jeans. The skirt may be lengthened to make it into a dress. Back and front are smocked but the back may be gathered into the yoke without the embroidery. It can also be made in plain material, when smocking transfers will be needed.

Materials

270 × 91 cm (3¼ yd × 36 in) gingham with 3 mm (⅛ in) checks
1 skein of stranded embroidery cotton in each of four colours, light, medium, dark and contrast
Smocking transfers if required, 2 for front and back each 62 × 11 cm (24½ × 4½ in) and 2 for sleeves each 37 × 16 cm (14½ × 6½ in), with dots and rows 6 mm (¼ in) apart. There should be 19 rows of 99 dots on the larger ones and 26 rows of 59 dots on the smaller ones, including an extra row at top and bottom on each
The original uses yellow gingham with white, orange, brown and blue-green embroidery

back view (same as front)

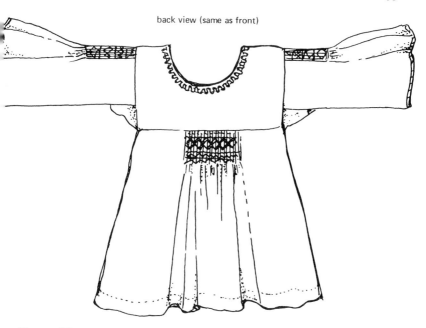

Figure 88

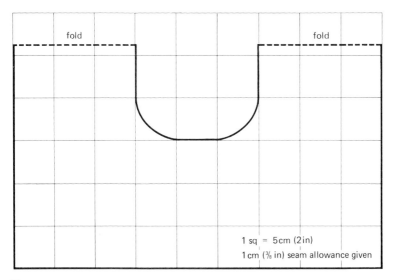

1 sq = 5cm (2in)
1 cm (⅜ in) seam allowance given

Figure 89

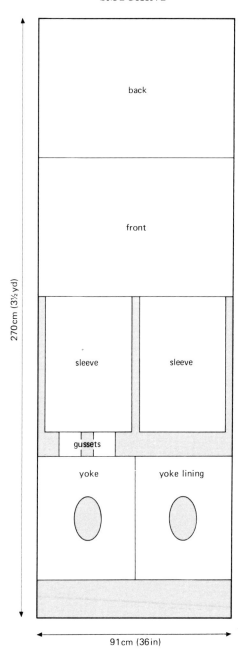

Figure 90

Measurements

To fit 81–91 cm (32–36 in) bust; length from top of shoulder, 81 cm (32 in); sleeve seam 33 cm (13 in).

Cutting out

1 cm (⅜ in) seam allowance has been given. Cut back and front each 91 × 63 cm (36 × 25 in), two sleeves each 61 × 38 cm (24 × 15 in), two gussets each 10 cm (4 in) square, two yokes according to pattern (one for lining).

Smocking preparation

Straighten the top and bottom edges of each piece for front, back and sleeves. Fold each in half lengthways and press in crease for centre. The smocking for back and front covers areas approximately 30 cm (12 in) *each side* of centre crease and 11 cm (4⅜ in) down from raw edge, including 1 cm (⅜ in) for seam allowance. Smocking for sleeves covers areas approximately 18 cm (7 in) *each side* of centre crease and 16 cm (6⅜ in) down. Apply transfers to wrong side with top row 3 mm (⅛ in) below raw edge, or gather by picking up light squares on wrong side of fabric, on alternate rows only, starting 3 mm (⅛ in) below raw edge. There should be 19 gathering threads on front and back panels and 26 on sleeve panels, including an extra row at top and bottom to help in making up only. Draw up back and front threads to measure 15 cm (6 in) and sleeve threads to 7.5 cm (3 in). Check that there are 98 pleats on front and back and 58 on each sleeve and adjust number if necessary.

Embroidery

The extra rows at top and bottom are omitted in the smocking instructions. Use six strands in the needle. Follow the diagram down to gathering thread 10, working the cable groups over pleats 8 to 3 in the centre of the diamond patterns in contrast thread, and carrying it loosely across the back between groups. The pattern should be repeated twelve times in all. *To continue the pattern place the next cable row halfway between gathering threads 10 and 11 to correspond with the cable row worked at the top of this trellis band. Begin diamond stitch using contrast colour on gathering thread 11 and continue to follow the diagram down to gathering thread 6,* ending on the fifteenth

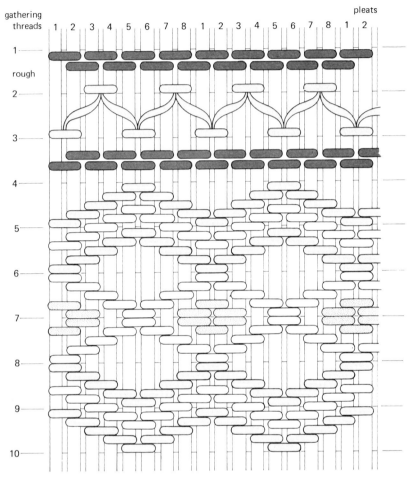

Figure 91

gathering thread on the panel. Leave half a space, then work a single row of contrasting colour trellis down to halfway between threads 16 and 17.

Sleeves Follow the diagram down to gathering thread 6, having 7 repeats along the row. Omit the two single trellis rows between threads 6 and 8. Work the triple trellis rows shown between threads 8 to 10, adding the isolated cable groups in contrast colour in the centre of the diamond shape just formed. Follow the instructions between * and * on the back and front panels placing first of these between the next two gathering threads, then work the single trellis row between gathering threads 6 and 7 on the diagram, also the triple trellis shown between threads 4 and 6. To finish, work a cable row halfway between the next two gathering threads, and repeat the diamond stitch, cable and two

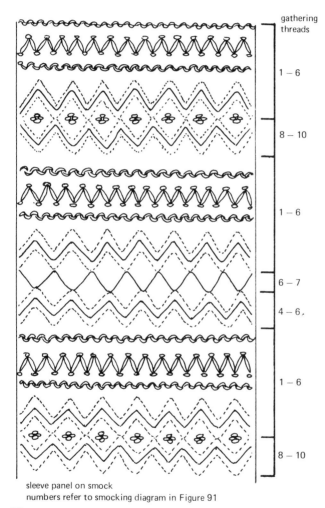

gathering
threads

1 — 6

8 — 10

1 — 6

6 — 7

4 — 6.

1 — 6

8 — 10

sleeve panel on smock
numbers refer to smocking diagram in Figure 91

Figure 92

triple trellis rows with cable groups embroidered at the top of the sleeve panel. See Figure 92 for the appearance of this panel.

To make up
Withdraw all gathering threads except the top one on each piece.

Yoke   With right sides together, tack yoke lining to yoke round neckline and stitch. Snip into seam allowance round curves, turn yoke lining to inside. Tack layers together round neck and press.

Front and back   With right sides together, pin the centre of the front to the centre of one lower edge on yoke, then tack in place matching side edges of yoke and front and taking 1 cm (⅜ in) seam on each piece so that the join will fall just above the top row of smocking. Sew the back to the yoke in the same way.

Sleeves   Join gusset to each sleeve as described for the smock dress on p. 125. Turn a very narrow hem at the bottom edge of each sleeve. Pin centre of smocking to centre of side edges of yoke with right sides together, tack and stitch as for back and front, continuing seam along remaining edges of gusset (see Figure 93).

Figure 93

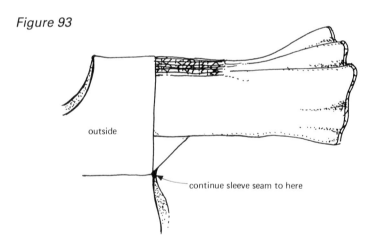

outside

continue sleeve seam to here

To complete   Join side seams on front and back. Turn yoke lining seam allowance to inside on all straight edges and slip stitch to hide all raw edges. Turn up a hem of approximately 5 cm (2 in) round lower edge of smock. The neck edge of the yoke may be decorated by a line of stitchery. A suggestion is shown in Figure 94. Work two parallel rows of back stitch in dark colour, each

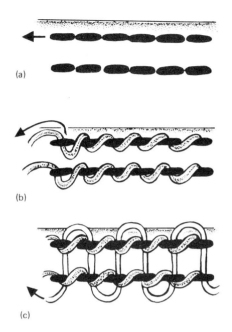

Figure 94

stitch about 6 mm (¼ in) long. On the outer curves the stitches will have to be a little larger (a). Whip each stitch with medium colour (b), and finally interlace rows with light colour (c). In Figure 94 the whipping and interlacing is shown looser than it would be worked.

SKIRT WITH TAPERED BACK AND FRONT PANELS

A flowery skirt always looks pretty for summer and the smocking can pick up the colours of the print. It is essential to use a yellow transfer if the material is light in colour; because the panels are tapered the dots not used may show through the material if they are blue.

Materials

250 × 114 cm or 260 × 91 cm (2¾ yd × 45 in or 2⅝ yd × 36 in) wide cotton/polyester material
1 skirt placket zip 20 cm (8 in) long
2 hooks and eyes

Figure 95

Petersham ribbon 3 cm (1⅛ in) wide to fit waist plus 5 cm (2 in), or the equivalent in thick Vilene, belting or other skirt-band interlining
250 cm (2¾ yd) ribbon 2.5 cm (1 in) wide for waist sash
2 skeins each of stranded cotton in light, medium and dark
Smocking transfer 242 × 14 cm (95½ × 5½ in), with dots and rows 6 mm (¼ in) apart. There should be 371 dots and 22 rows on the transfer, including an extra row at top and bottom. Join transfers on the back with sticky tape to give required length where necessary
The original uses fine cream cotton/polyester with flower prints in shades of rust, brown, yellow ochre and denim blue, embroidered with pale rust, blue and brown

Measurements
242 cm (95½ in) all round hem; length 74 cm (29 in), adjustable; waist, adjustable.

Cutting out
2.5 cm (1 in) seam allowance on side edge, 1 cm (⅜ in) at waist edge and ample hem have been given. If using 114 cm (45 in) wide material, trim a strip 8 cm (3¼ in) from length of material measuring from one selvedge. If using 91 cm (36 in) material cut same width strip across the width of one end of the material.

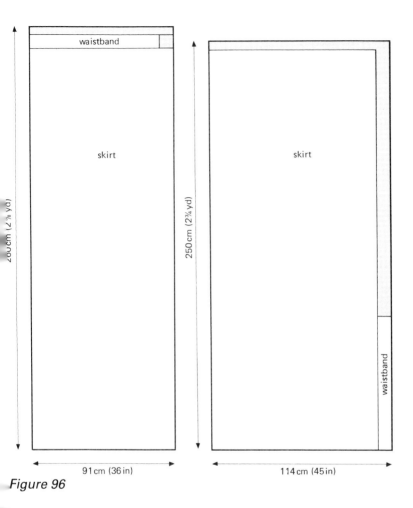

Figure 96

Trim either strip to required length of waistband plus 7 cm (2¾ in). For both widths of material trim the remainder to 247 cm (97½ in) long.

Smocking preparation

The skirt is smocked along the length of the material. Apply the transfer to the wrong side 1 cm (⅜ in) away from the selvedge, leaving approximately 2.5 cm (1 in) at both short ends for the side opening. Gather along the smocking dots with two or more lengths of cotton, making the break in each at the same place. You may like to make sure the thread will not snap by gathering with button-hole thread. Alternatively ordinary cotton may be

strengthened and made less liable to tangle by passing it along a
piece of beeswax or household wax candle. Draw up threads to
waist measurement. At the break or breaks in each row, pairs of
threads should be tied together as described for the baby's
bonnet on p. 45. There should be 370 pleats in the material.

Embroidery

The top and bottom threads are to help in the making up only
and are not included in the diagram. Use four strands in the
needle. There should be 46 repeats along the row. Follow the
diagram to the bottom of the second single trellis row between
gathering threads 4 and 5. All single trellis rows are worked in
dark colour. The colour arrangement of the triple rows is varied
to alternate between light–medium–light colours as on the first

Figure 97

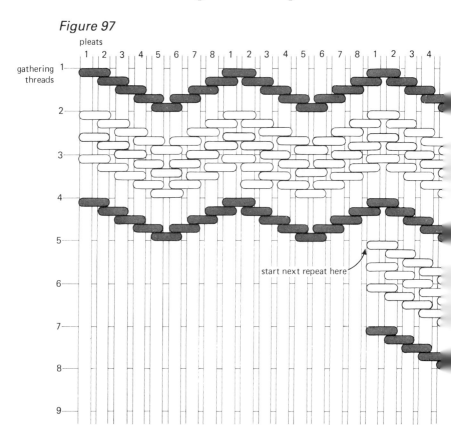

triple row between gathering threads 2 and 4, and medium–light–medium as on the second triple row between threads 5 and 7. After the second single trellis row has been worked, divide the work into halves for the back and front panels by marking with a safety pin, having 23 repeats in each half. On the second triple trellis row shown in Figure 97 between threads 5 and 7, count the first 16 pleats and leave these unworked, thus missing out the first two repeats, and continue to follow the diagram for nineteen repeats. Leave four repeats unworked, then embroider another nineteen repeats. For the third repeat of the triple trellis (not shown in Figure 97) leave out another two repeats at the beginning of the row and stitch fifteen repeats on back and front panels. Continue in this way having four less repeats on each panel every time the triple trellis row is worked until there are three repeats only on the sixth and last row (see Figure 98).

To make up

Withdraw all gathering threads except for the top one.

Side opening   With right sides together and taking a 2.5 cm (1 in) seam, tack short edges together for 21 cm (8¼ in), starting at the smocked edge. Machine stitch along the rest of the seam. Pin and tack the closed zip so that its teeth are underneath the tacked part of the seam and the pulling tag is 1.5 cm (½ in) below raw edge. Either back stitch by hand or machine stitch 6 mm (¼ in) either side of the seam and across the closed zip end.

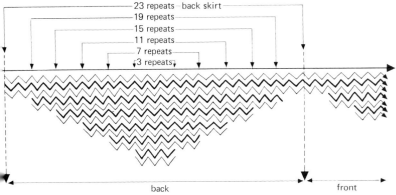

Figure 98

Waist band   Open zip. With right side of skirt facing and zip on the left side of the work, pin and tack waist band to skirt top, having right sides and raw edges together. Allow the short end to project 1 cm (⅜ in) on back opening edge and 6 cm (2½ in) on front opening edge (see Figure 99). Stitch seam and press waist band up, including lower raw edge of extension on front. Also press in 1 cm (⅜ in) on each short end. Tack petersham ribbon or Vilene stiffening to wrong side of waistband just above the seam, fold remainder of waistband to inside. Turn in seam allowance and slip stitch, including short ends. Top stitch 3 mm (⅛ in) from edge all round waistband. Sew hooks and eyes to fasten front extension in place. To slot ribbon sash in place on top of waistband make four button-holed loops at even intervals.

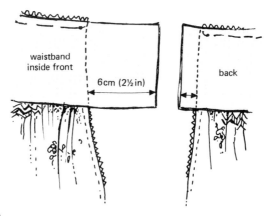

Figure 99

Hem   Try on the skirt and decide on its length. Trim and turn a 7.5 cm (3 in) hem, or decorate the lower edge in some way before hemming. You may like to add a band of ric-rac braid or three or four rows of spaced tucks, as on the skirt in the photograph.

SUN DRESS OR NIGHT DRESS

On hot days nothing could be cooler than this cotton dress which falls straight from the shoulders. The same design may be used for a fine cotton night dress, or a summer maternity dress. The smocking is worked on the front only, but if you want to smock

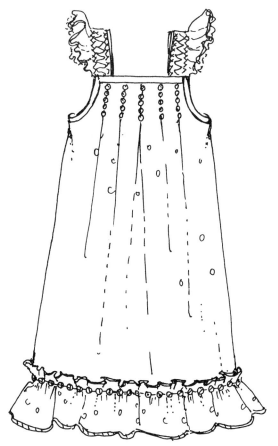

Figure 100

the back cut it the same width as the front. No smocking transfer is needed if you use seersucker fabric as the stripes in the weave serve as a guide when gathering.

Materials

250 × 114 cm (2¾ yd × 45 in) seersucker or plain cotton fabric
2 m (2¼ yd) narrow trimming
3 skeins stranded embroidery cotton in one colour
Smocking transfers if required, one 82 × 12 cm (32¼ × 4½ in) for front and two 71 × 4 cm (28 × 1½ in) for sleeve frills with dots 6 mm (¼ in) apart and rows 8 mm (⅜ in) apart (see p. 38).

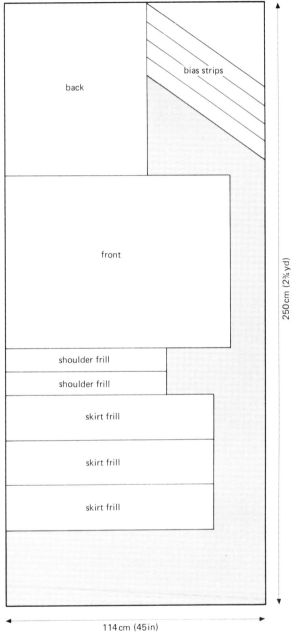

Figure 101

There should be 12 rows on the larger transfer and 4 on each of the smaller ones, including an extra row at top and bottom. The exact number of dots on each row does not matter

The original uses yellow seersucker with white dots, white embroidery and trimming

Measurements

To fit bust 81–92 cm (32–36 in); length 107 cm (42 in), adjustable.

Cutting out

1 cm (⅜ in) seam allowance has been given. Cut back 62 × 76 cm (24½ × 30 in) along the warp or stripe of the fabric. For plain fabric the length of 76 cm should be parallel to the selvedge. Cut front 100 × 76 cm (39½ × 30 in) along the warp. Cut two shoulder frills each 71 × 10 cm (28 × 4 in) along the warp and three skirt frills each 92 × 20 cm (36 × 8 in) also along the warp. Fold each shoulder frill in half across the width and cut out following Figure 102. Make a pattern of the armhole (Figure 103). Fold the back in half lengthwise and with fold on the left cut armhole from the top right hand corner of the doubled fabric.

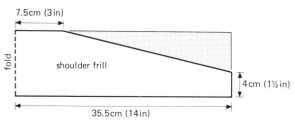

Figure 102

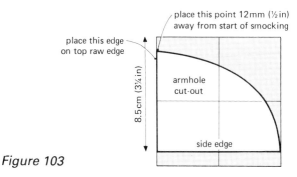

Figure 103

Spread out the front in single thickness with right side facing and
cut out one armhole only from the top left corner. To indicate the
inner edge of the right armhole insert a pin 8.5 cm (3¼ in) away
from the right edge; do not cut out this armhole yet.

Smocking preparation

Turn a very narrow hem on the shaped edge of each sleeve frill.
The seersucker has crinkly stripes on the weave each approximately 8 mm (⅜ in) wide with plain weave stripes half as wide.
The woven spots can be used as a guide for the placing the rows,
or you may rule these lightly with a pencil if the fabric is plain.
Take one gathering stitch in the centre of the crinkly stripe and
one in the centre of the plain stripe. The side you are working on
will then become the wrong side.

Place the top row of gathering on each piece 3 mm (⅛ in)
away from the raw edge. Stitch twelve gathering rows on the
front and four on each shoulder frill, beginning and ending each
within 1 cm (⅜ in) of each end on shoulder frills. On front begin
12 mm (½ in) away from inner edge of cut-out armhole and end
same width away from pin to indicate the other armhole. Pull up
shoulder frills to 24 cm (9½ in) and on front to 25 cm (10 in). If
using transfers, apply to wrong side and gather up in the same
way.

Embroidery

The top and bottom gathering threads are not shown (Figure
104).

Front Follow Figure 104. Work a double cable stitch along
gathering thread 1, then begin the double trellis row just below
gathering thread 2. As the sides of this design are tapered you
will need a complete repeat to finish the end of the row so that
each side will match. Work to the right-hand side and end off
this row with a complete pattern, finishing as near to the pin as
possible. Continue with the pattern as set until you have worked
the top diamond row between gathering threads 4 and 5. On the
next diamond row begin and end on the second repeat from
either side, as shown in Figure 104. Work two more rows of
diamond stitch omitting one repeat either end as shown. The
first and last eight pleats will now be left unworked. Begin the

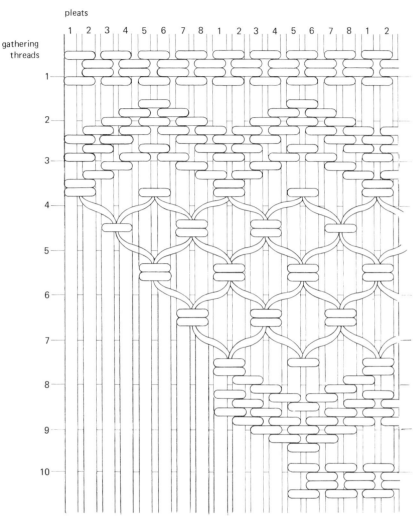

Figure 104

triple trellis row on the ninth pleat, and the final double cable on the thirteenth pleat.

Shoulder frills No diagram is given for these. Begin with a double cable row between gathering threads 1 and 2, then work a diamond stitch row touching the lower of these down to halfway between threads 2 and 3. Work a pairing diamond stitch row down to halfway between threads 3 and 4, and finish with another double cable row.

To make up

Withdraw all gathering threads except the top one on each piece. From remainder of material, cut and join enough bias strips to give a length of approximately 170 cm (67 in).

Front   Cut the remaining armhole, placing the inner edge 12 mm (½ in) away from the right end of the smocking. You may need to trim a little away from the right-side edge. With right sides together, pin a 2.5 cm (1 in) wide strip of self binding along the upper raw edge, stretching it slightly, and back stitch by hand, taking a seam of 1 cm (⅜ in) and catching the binding to the top of the smocking pleats only so as not to flatten them. Turn it over to the wrong side, fold in the raw edge and slip stitch.

Back   To reduce the fullness above the armhole, make an inverted pleat at centre back and two other pleats equally on either side. Insert a pin to mark centre of neck edge and another 4 cm (1½ in) on either side. With right side facing, fold material so that these two outer pins are now touching in the centre, thus making an inverted pleat. Reduce the measurement of the neck edge to 25 cm (10 in) by making two more single pleats on either side of the centre about 4 cm (1½ in) apart. The folded edge of each pleat should face into the centre. Pin and tack each pleat straight down for 10 cm (4 in) from raw edge, which is then bound as for front.

Armholes   Join side seams with right sides together, taking 1 cm (⅜ in) seam. Bind armholes as before, taking the strips over the ends of the front and back binding. Turn in the raw ends in line with the upper edge of these and oversew to close.

Shoulder frills   Bind the straight edges. Oversew the short ends to neaten. Pin frills to upper edges of binding on front and back, so that outer shaped edge will be in line with armhole binding, and back stitch in place on the inside.

Skirt frill With right sides together, join short ends and turn a very narrow hem on both edges. Using strong thread, run a gathering thread around the frill 1.5 cm (⅝ in) away from one edge. Adjusting length of dress if necessary, press up 6 mm (¼ in) to right side so that lower edges will be neatened. Draw up frill to fit dress, and working on right side tack and stitch gathering over pressed-up edge.

Trimming Sew trimming on right side over skirt frill gathering thread and over stitched pleat folds on back.

SLEEVELESS WAISTCOAT

In peasant designs the main feature of a garment is often placed at the back where it can be seen to its best advantage. The smocking on the back of this waistcoat, influenced by bright peasant colouring, shows off your work beautifully and has the added attraction of shaping the garment perfectly to the figure. A variety of colours is suggested but you may like to carry it out in only three or four. Bands at the bottom are also optional, and the length of the garment can be varied.

Materials

Estimate length required, subtract 10 cm (4 in) if bands are to be added, and allow twice this length in 150 cm (60 in) wool or synthetic jersey material
For bands, binding and rouleau: 40 cm (½ yd) black, 30 cm (12 in) pink, 10 cm (4 in) scarlet nylon jersey material 150 cm (60 in) wide
For binding and rouleau alone: 20 cm (8 in) black and 20 cm (8 in) pink same-width jersey
1 skein in each of five colours of tapisserie wool
Chenille needle
Smocking transfer 73.5 × 43.5 cm (29 × 17 in) with dots 12 mm (2 in) apart and rows 8 mm (⅜ in) apart (see p. 38). There should be 59 dots in each of 46 rows including an extra row top and bottom
The original uses aubergine synthetic jersey with black binding, scarlet and bright pink bands at the bottom, embroidery in black, mauve, blue-green, bright pink and orange

back view   front view

Figure 105

Measurements

To fit 81–86 cm/86–91/91–97 cm (32–34/34–36/36–38 in) bust;
length at centre back 119 cm (47 in), adjustable.

Cutting out

1 cm (⅜ in) seam allowance has been given. The pattern shown
is in size 86–91 cm (34–36 in). For a size *smaller* cut off 12 mm (½

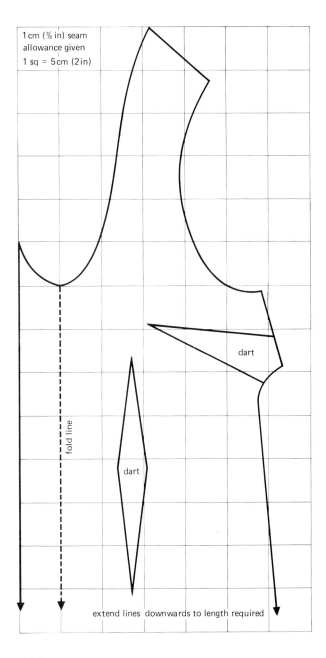

1 cm (⅜ in) seam allowance given
1 sq = 5 cm (2 in)

fold line

dart

dart

extend lines downwards to length required

Figure 106

in) at side back and fronts. For a size *larger* add on the same
amount in the same places. Adjust bust dart to measure 15 cm (6
in) in both sizes. Cut out two fronts as given allowing for the fact
that the bands at the bottom will measure 18 cm (7 in) altogether
when the garment is completed. Transfer all markings. Do not
cut out darts. For the back cut a piece of material 81 cm (32 in)
wide by desired length minus bands. This will be shaped when

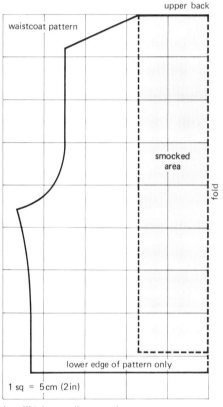

Figure 107

the smocking is complete, so for the present cut a pattern in stiff
paper only. For the bands, cut strips all 145 cm (57 in) long as
follows: black, 22 cm (9 in); pink 12 cm (4¾ in); scarlet 5 cm (2
in); main colour jersey 7 cm (2¾ in).

full-length version with bands   119 cm (47 in)

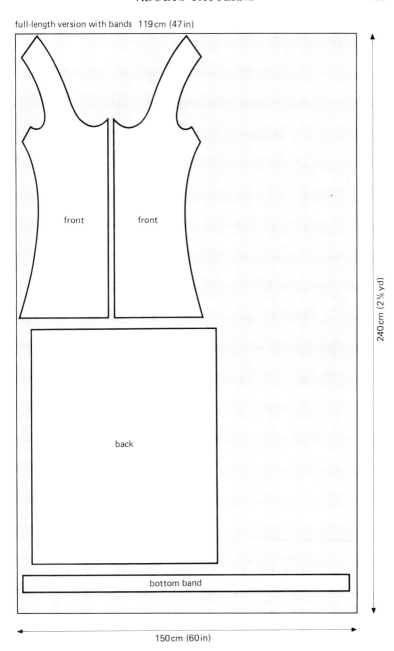

240 cm (2 ⅝ yd)

150 cm (60 in)

Figure 108

Smocking preparation

Fold material for back in half along length and crease or tack along fold for 41 cm (16 in) from one edge to mark centre. Apply transfer to centre of wrong side of material, with the top row 1 cm (⅜ in) away from the straightened raw edge. If there is difficulty in making the dots visible tack transfer in place and sew through paper, afterwards tearing it away. Gather and draw up threads to 18 cm (7 in). There should be 58 pleats to contain an exact number of repeats.

Embroidery

Use a chenille needle, which has a large eye and a point. The top and bottom gathering threads are to assist in making up only and are omitted in the instructions. Follow Figure 109, working rope stitch above and below gathering thread 1 in black, and cable stitch in between in mauve. Subsequent rows of these stitches are worked in the same colours throughout. Using bright pink, start the combined cable and diamond stitch on gathering thread 3 and repeat the pattern seven times in all. Work groups of four stitches in black as shown over pleats 1 and 2 in each repeat, finishing off at the back after each group to retain elasticity. Keep to the same colours for these stitches also. The rows between gathering threads 6 and 10 inclusive are varied in colour each of the four times they are worked.

One   First group of trellis rows 1, 3, 4 and 6 in bright pink; trellis rows 2 and 5 and centre diamond stitch row in blue-green; groups of double stitches over pleats 1 and 2, 5 and 6 in each repeat in orange, carrying thread loosely along at the back in between each repeat.

Two   First group in orange, second group in mauve, double stitches in blue-green.

Three   First group in blue-green, second group in orange, double stitches in bright pink.

Four   First group in mauve, second in bright pink, double stitches in blue-green.

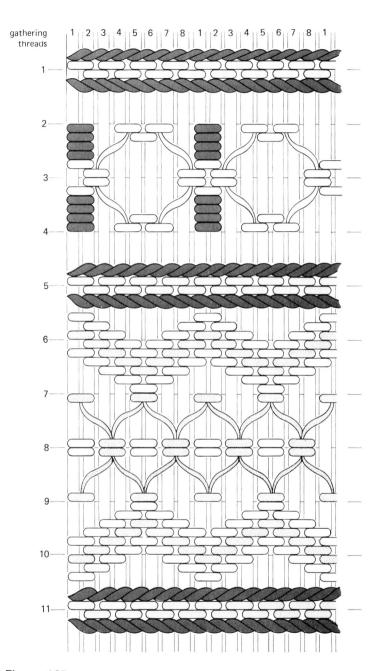

Figure 109

Repeat rows over gathering threads 1 to 10 inclusive four times, then repeat rows 1 to 4 once more over forty-four gathering threads.

To make up

Back Withdraw all gathering threads except the top one. Pin the paper pattern for the back to the finished work, placing the centre fold carefully to the centre of the smocking. Cut out according to the pattern down to a level with the bottom of the smocked area, then leave the remainder of the sides uncut.

Front Dart fronts. Press side darts downwards. Cut along fold of dart on the inside on front darts and press darts open. Join fronts and back on shoulder and side seams, press seams open.

Bands Taking 1 cm (³⁄₈ in) seam throughout, join the four bands with right sides together on long edges in the following order: scarlet, main-colour jersey, bright pink, black. With right sides together, join free edge of scarlet band to lower edge of waistcoat. Press seams open and ensure that front edges of bands are straight. Top stitch close to seams on right side if desired. Fold 5 cm (2 in) to inside of fronts, tack in place at top neckline edge and press along length. Slip stitch in place up to top edge of black (lowest) band. Turn this band to the inside of the waistcoat so that a border of 1.5 cm (⁵⁄₈ in) remains visible on the outside; the remainder will form a facing on the inside. Turn in its remaining free long edge and slip stitch to join of top band to lower edge of waistcoat. Trim short edges of facing to 1 cm (³⁄₈ in) and slip stitch to front folded edges (see Figures 110a and b).

To complete From remainder of black jersey cut and join sufficient 4-cm (1½-in) bias strips to bind neck and armholes – approximately 230 cm (2½ yd). From remainder of pink jersey cut and join sufficient 4-cm (1½ in) bias strips to give a length of approximately 150 cm (60 in) and make a rouleau strip. See p. 35 for binding and rouleau instructions.

To lace fronts, make eyelet holes 1 cm (³⁄₈ in) from folded edge on each front, having top one 1.5 cm (⁵⁄₈ in) away from neckline edge and remainder at 5 cm (12½ in) intervals. Make eyelet

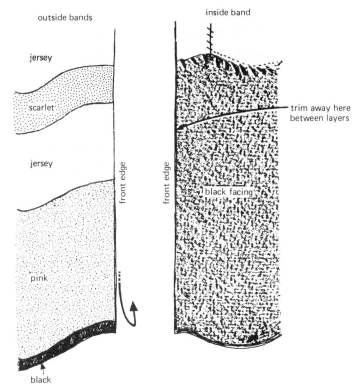

outside bands

jersey

scarlet

jersey

front edge

pink

black

inside band

front edge

trim away here
between layers

black facing

Figure 110

holes by inserting stiletto point or point of scissors through material, then twist to enlarge to a small hole about 6 mm (¼ in) across. A knitting needle may be used to enlarge the hole. Overcast closely and tightly round the hole with matching cotton. The waistcoat may also be fastened with buttons and corresponding loops of thread which have been button-hole stitched to strengthen them, or it may be tied by three or four matching pairs of ribbon lengths sewn to the fronts.

TRADITIONAL SMOCK DRESS

This dress is based on the original smock worn by countrymen, and uses the same method of construction. It also features traditional Dorset wheel hand-made buttons.

Figure 111

Materials

300 × 114 cm (3¼ yd × 45 in) or 330 × 91 cm (3½ yd × 36 in) cotton material
2 balls Sylko Perlé no 8 or 7 skeins stranded embroidery cotton
6 plastic curtain rings 2 cm (¾ in) diameter
2 press studs
16 cm (6¼ in) narrow elastic
1 smocking transfer for front 59 × 34 cm (23¼ × 13½ in), exact number of rows and dots does not matter
2 smocking transfers for top sleeves 11.5 × 10 cm (4½ × 4 in) and 2 for bottom sleeves 32 × 11 cm (12½ × 4¼ in) with dots 6 mm (¼ in) apart and rows 8 mm (⅜ in) apart (see p. 38). There should be 11 rows of 19 dots each on the top sleeve transfers and 11 rows of 51 dots each on the bottom sleeve transfers, including an extra row at top and bottom. Join transfers on the back with sticky tape if necessary
Original uses caramel colour heavy cotton with cream embroidery and buttons

Measurements

To fit bust 82–92 cm (32–36 in) adjustable; length from shoulder 118 cm (46 in); sleeve seam 40 cm (16 in) plus 10 cm (4 in) underarm gusset.

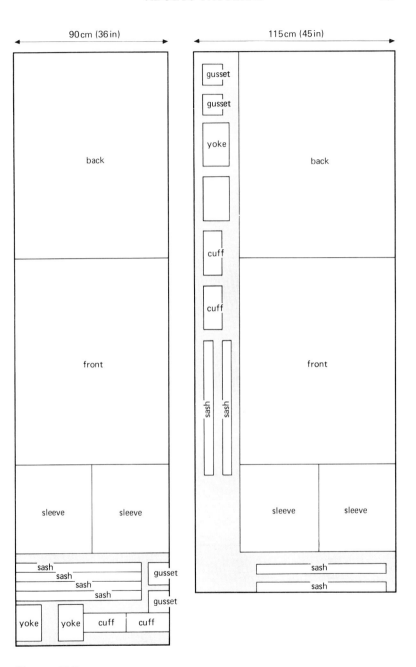

Figure 112

Cutting out

1 cm (⅜ in) seam allowance has been given. Cut front and back 114 × 90 cm (45 × 36 in); two sleeves 51 × 45 cm (20 × 17¾ in); two gussets 12 cm (4¾ in) square; two cuffs 24 × 10 cm (9½ × 4 in); two yokes 23 × 16 cm (9 × 6¼ in); four sashes 76 × 5 cm (30 × 2 in). To adapt the pattern to fit bust 92–97 cm (36–38 in) add 12 mm (½ in) to side seams of front and back, sleeve underarm edges and yoke armhole edge and use material 114 cm (45 in) wide.

Smocking preparation

Take the pieces for the front back and sleeves and make sure the edges are straight by pulling threads and trimming to correspond. Fold front in half lengthways and press along fold for about 36 cm (14½ in) from one edge. Open out. Use crease to centre transfer on wrong side of material, with top line of transfer just below raw edge. Pin in place and iron off. Apply transfers to wrong sides of sleeves in the same way. Gather on smocking dots and draw up bodice gathers to 16 cm (6¼ in), top sleeve to 3 cm (1¼ in), bottom sleeve to 8 cm (3¼ in).

Embroidery

The first gathering thread helps in making up only and is not included in Figure 113. There will also be one or two rows left over at the bottom.

Bodice   Work cable stitch on gathering thread 1 and rope stitch halfway in between threads 1 and 2. Begin the feather stitch, which is worked from right to left, by coming up on the right of pleat A as shown in the numerals along the top line of Figure 113. Insert the needle just below the place where you came up and take a horizontal stitch through pleats A and B, thus making a loop round the needle. Continue to advance one pleat every stitch, repeating the pattern regularly after pleat D (see p. 22). Continue until the cable row on gathering thread 7 has been completed, then for the next row count to the centre pleat and use the method described on p. 20 to centre the trellis halfway between gathering threads 7 and 8. When the four trellis rows have been worked, repeat them all once more, having the fifth row just below so that its top stitch touches the lowest stitch of the fourth row. Using the same spacing repeat the cable and rope

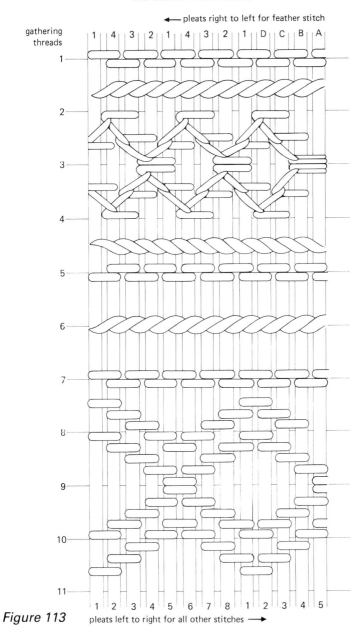

gathering threads

← pleats right to left for feather stitch

Figure 113 pleats left to right for all other stitches ⟶

stitch on gathering threads 14 and 15; leave one space and, starting on gathering thread 16, repeat the whole design once

single feather stitch

Figure 114

more, then work the feather stitch panel only, ending with a row of cable stitch as on gathering thread 5. Work one row of single feather stitch down each side of the panel (see Figure 114).

Top sleeve   Starting on the second gathering thread work the design as given over gathering threads 1 to 9.

Bottom sleeve   Starting on the second gathering thread work the design from gathering thread 6 to the bottom, then repeat the four trellis rows once more.

To make up

Withdraw gathering threads.

Back   Take 1 cm (⅜ in) seam throughout the garment. To mark centre fold the material in half lengthways and press along the

traditional smock dress

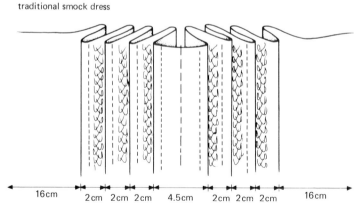

Figure 115

fold from one edge to 31 cm (12¼ in). The centre panel on the
back is now pleated to equal the smocked panel on the front, so
that 16 cm (6¼ in) is left plain at either side of the material.
Alternatively it may be smocked to match the front. A suggestion
for pleating is shown in Figure 115. Tack and press the pleats,
then top stitch evenly approximately 6 mm (¼ in) from the edge
of each pleat. To emphasize them work a row of single feather
stitch under the line of top stitching.

Front On inside of smocked panel catch a piece of elastic with
herring bone stitch across the bottom, to hold the gathers in
place (see Figures 24 and 71).

Yoke Place the yokes lengthwise between the back and front
pieces, right sides together and stitch (see Figure 116). Bind
round the entire neck with 4 cm (1⅝ in) wide crossway strips cut
from remnants.

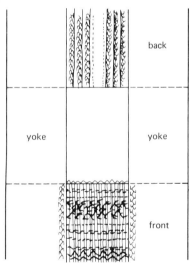

Figure 116

Sleeves First add the gusset. With right sides together pin one
edge to top edge of sleeve and stitch (Figure 117). With right
sides together fold sleeve in half lengthways and pin together so
that gusset is folded diagonally and edge A-B is now pinned to
the other sleeve edge (Figure 118). Leaving 8 cm (3¼ in) open at
the wrist end, stitch the entire seam towards the gusset. Press
seam allowance back along opening and stitch down.

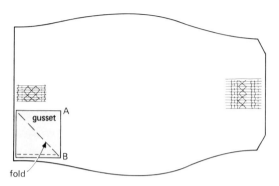

Figure 117

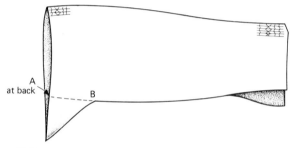

Figure 118

Cuffs Fold cuffs in half, right sides together, and stitch across short ends making extension as shown (Figure 119). Turn right side out. On outside of sleeve, pin cuffs to sleeves, right sides together and raw edges level, having cuff extension on the left for left sleeve and on the right for right sleeve (Figure 120). Stitch lower edge of cuff to sleeve, press seam downwards. Fold cuff to inside and turn in raw edge, slip stitch to sleeve.

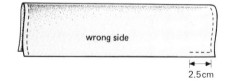

Figure 119

Setting in sleeves and side seams With right sides together matching centre of top smocking to centres of yokes, sew sleeves to edges of dress front, yokes and back, then close side seams.

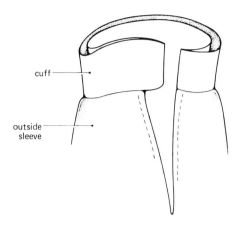

cuff

outside
sleeve

Figure 120

Sashes Fold each in half lengthways and stitch leaving one end
open. Turn to right side, oversew open end together. Stitch one
to either side at bottom of front and back panels.

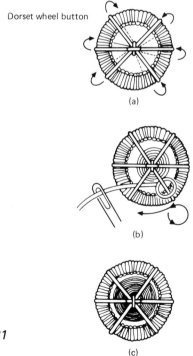

Dorset wheel button

(a)

(b)

(c)

Figure 121

Hem   Turn up hem and work a row of single feather stitch 2 cm
(¾ in) away from folded edge. Sew press studs to fasten cuffs.

Buttons

Dorset wheel hand-made buttons give a charming finish. To
make one, button-hole stitch all round a curtain ring using the
same embroidery thread as for the smocking, then turn the
button-holing so that the ridge of the stitches is now inside the
ring. Secure a new long thread about 2 m (2¼ yd) with a firm
back stitch at the back and wrap round the ring, shifting the
thread a little at each turn until there are six even spokes. Bring
the needle up in the middle and secure with a firm cross stitch
where spokes overlap. Now work a spider's web from centre
outwards by back stitching over one spoke, forward under two
and so on. Leave a small gap at the edge (see Figure 121a, b and
c). Sew one button over each sash attachment and one over press
studs on cuffs.

6

PATTERNS USING CANADIAN OR RUCHED SMOCKING

The following four designs all use the same method of smocking. Here the fullness of the material is not reduced by gathering but by drawing points of material together to give a decorative pleated finish on the right side. The work is purely textural and not elastic. No preliminary gathering threads are used and it is simple to make your own smocking graph, or make use of ready-woven squares in the case of the sunhat.

SQUARE CUSHION

Materials

100 × 122 cm (1¼ yd × 48 in) lightweight furnishing material, velvet or synthetic mixture (choose something with body which will not crush
Cushion pad 45 cm (18 in) square
2 m (2¼ yd) thick piping cord
Zip fastener 30 cm (12 in) long

Measurements

42 cm (16½ in) square

Cutting out

Cut a piece of material 68 cm (27 in) square for the front and two pieces each 44 × 22 cm (17½ × 8½ in) for the back. From the remainder of the material cut and join sufficient bias strips each 5 cm (2 in) wide to give a joined length of 2 m (2¼ yd).

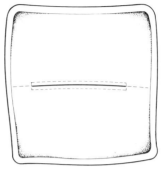

back view of square smocked cushion

Figure 122

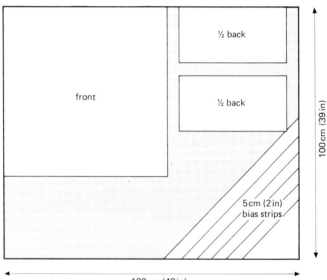

Figure 123   122 cm (48 in)

Smocking preparation

Each vertical line of smocking is worked on the wrong side of the
fabric over 3 rows of dots spaced 2.5 cm (1 in) apart. Since in this
design the smocking lines are adjacent to each other each line
occupies two vertical rows of squares formed by the dots. See
Figure 124 for further explanation.

To make your own smocking chart either rule a grid directly
onto the wrong side of the material using a soft pencil or

water-soluble embroidery pencil, or pierce holes in a ruled piece of brown paper or dressmaker's graph paper and dot the material through the holes.

Make a grid in the centre of the 68-cm (27-in) square of material on the wrong side of the fabric. There should be a margin of 9 cm (3½ in) all round the grid which should be 50 cm (20 in) square and have 21 rows of dots or 20 squares each way spaced at 2.5-cm (1-in) intervals.

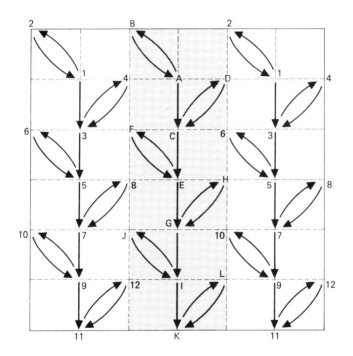

Figure 124

Smocking

Use thread double throughout. Make a large knot on the end of the thread. Following Figure 125 start in the top left-hand corner of the grid. Pick up dot 1, then pick up dot 2, go back to dot 1 and

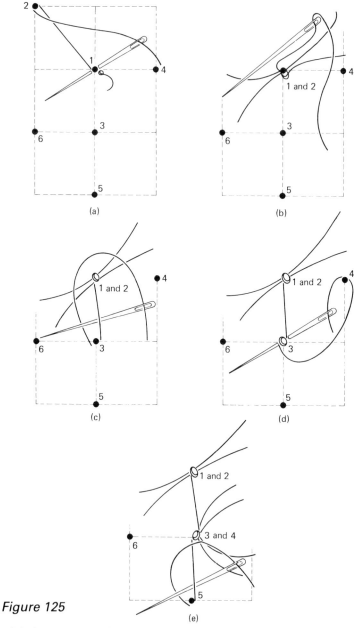

Figure 125

pick it up again (Figure 125a). Pull dots 1 and 2 together and knot securely by making a loop of the thread above the stitches and passing the needle under the stitches and through the loop (Figure 125b). Be careful not to catch the fabric as you do this or the stitch will show on the right side. Pick up dot 3. Keeping the fabric completely flat between dots 1 and 3, make a knotting loop as before but do not draw up the thread (Figure 125c). Pick up dot 4, go back to dot 3 and pick it up again (Figure 125d). Pull dots 3 and 4 together and make a knotting loop. Pick up dot 5 and knot the thread, keeping the fabric flat as at dot 3 (Figure 125e). Pick up dot 6, pull up to dot 5 and knot. Continue in this way down the whole line, working alternately in a straight line down the middle and diagonally out to right and left. After vertical stitches, leave the fabric flat; pull it up after diagonal stitches. Knot the thread after every complete movement, and end with a diagonal stitch to the right. Finish off with two or three back stitches and begin again at the top of the second line, in the third row of squares from the left. Continue until all ten lines are complete.

To make up

Front You will now find that pleats have formed all round the edge. Pin these down evenly and tack in position, checking that each side measures 40 cm (16 in) (see Figure 126).

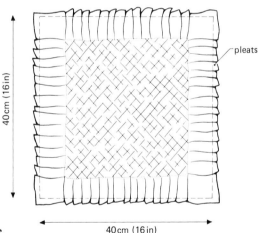

Figure 126

40 cm (16 in)

40 cm (16 in)

pleats

Piping Piping is optional. Fold one short end of the bias strip to the wrong side for about 1 cm (⅜ in) to neaten the end. With right side facing, fold the bias round the piping cord with raw edges together and tack to enclose it, as shown in Figure 127.

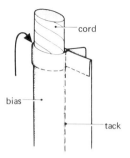

Figure 127

With right side of cushion front facing and raw edges of front and piping together, tack the piping all round the sides. To join the ends together, trim the cord and catch the ends together as much as possible to make the length continuous, then trim the bias strip so that there is a surplus of approximately 1 cm (⅜ in); fold to inside and slip stitch folded ends together (see Figure 128).

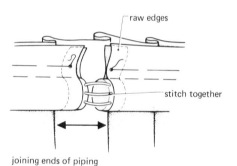

Figure 128   joining ends of piping
                    (shown loosened)

Back   With right sides together and pile running in the same direction if you are using velvet, tack long sides together with 1.5 cm (⅝ in) seam. Machine along tacking for 7 cm (2¾ in), leave a space of 30 cm (12 in) for zip. Machine along remainder of seam. Steam press seam open. Tack zip in position. Working on the right side top stitch 6 mm (¼ in) away from seam all round zip. Remove tackings.

To complete   Place right sides of back and front together with piping sandwiched in between, tack and machine stitch close to the piping cord using a piping foot if you have one. If not, a firm back stitch by hand is just as effective.

ROUND CUSHION

In this cushion the lines of smocking are spaced apart from each other to give a less tightly plaited effect. The continuous circle of smocking forms the side and the resulting pleats make the top and bottom.

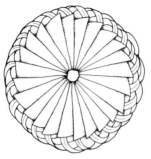

Figure 129

back and front views the same

Materials

100 × 122 cm (1¼ yd × 48 in) furnishing material, as for square cushion
2 button moulds or flat buttons approximately 2.5 cm (1 in) diameter
Matching button-hole thread
45 cm (18 in) diameter round cushion pad

Measurements

40.5 cm (16 in) diameter; 10 cm (4 in) thick.

Cutting out

All measurements must be taken accurately. Straighten both ends of the material by pulling threads. Cut a piece 8 cm (3¼ in) from one end across the width. Cut the remainder of the material along the length to give two pieces each 92 × 61 cm (36 × 24 in). There is no cutting diagram.

Smocking preparation

As suggested for the square cushion make a chart 89 × 20 cm (35 × 8 in) having 36 lines of 9 dots or 35 rows of 8 squares spaced at 2.5 cm (1 in) intervals. Pierce holes through the dots and mark the material on the wrong side. Alternatively rule a grid directly onto the fabric. There should be a margin of 20.5 cm (8¼ in) on either side of the grid down the length and 12 mm (½ in) at either end. With right sides together, taking seams of 12 mm (½ in), join short ends of material, carefully aligning dots so that seams run through a row of dots on each piece and the smocking can be worked in a continuous round.

Smocking

Following Figure 130 work the smocking in the same way as for the square cushion but notice that the three lines are each spaced 2.5 cm (1 in) away from each other.

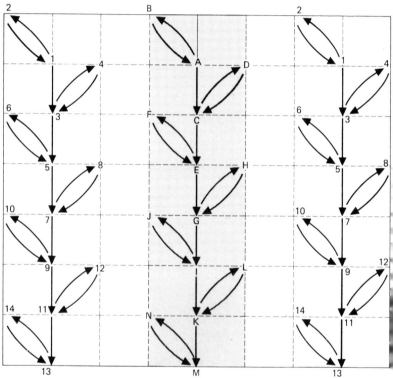

Figure 130

To make up

Using a strong thread, fasten the end firmly 6 mm (¼ in) from one free edge of the fabric. With right side facing form the first pleat with your fingers according to the way it results from the smocking. Stab straight through the fold about 6 mm (¼ in) from the edge. Continue pleating and stitching evenly all round the cushion (see Figure 131). Draw up the thread very tightly through the resulting series of concertina folds and fasten off very securely. Insert pad and pleat the other side in the same way.

Figure 131

Cover the buttons or button moulds with the spare fabric and sew to the centre on either side. The pleats may be set if you wish by allowing a steam iron to hover just above the surface of the work.

GINGHAM SUN HAT FOR CHILD OR ADULT

Two sizes are given. The first will fit a child of about four years upwards; the second will fit a teenager or adult. The hat will stretch to fit when worn. Measurements for the smaller hat are given first. When only one measurement is given it applies to both sizes.

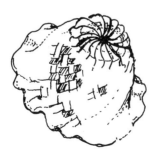

Figure 132

Materials

50 × 91 cm (19¾ × 36 in) or 100 × 91 cm (1¼ yd × 36 in) gingham with 2.5 cm (1 in) squares
or 50 × 114 cm (19¾ × 45 in) for both sizes gingham, also with 2.5 cm (1 in) squares

Measurements

To fit head approximately 53/58 cm (21/23 in) round brow.

To cut out

Cut gingham on the squares to measure 45.5 × 82 cm (18 × 32 in)/48 × 96.5 cm (19 × 38 in).

Smocking preparation

Join short edges, matching squares exactly to give 30/36 or an even number of squares all round the width. Trim seams to 1 cm (⅜ in) and neaten. Press to one side.

Brim On one long edge press 8 cm (3¼ in) or three squares to one side, then turn in square and hem by hand. Catch the layers together at the intersection of the squares and halfway between them, sliding the needle inside the fold of the hem between stitches. This will ensure that the hemming does not show on the finished work.

Smocking

Place the material wrong side facing with the raw edge at the top and the seam to the left. Knot the end of the thread. Follow the

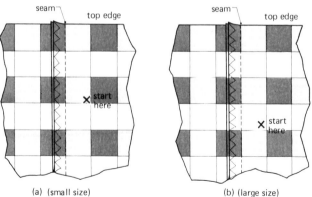

(a) (small size)   (b) (large size)

Figure 133

instructions for Canadian smocking given on p. 129, using the gingham squares as a ready-made grid. The first stitch will be taken in the square marked in Figure 133a for the smaller size and in Figure 133b for the larger. Continue working downwards until you reach the upper edge of the brim, ending with a diagonal movement to the left. Finish off the thread. The next row of smocking will occupy the adjacent two rows of squares to the right. Continue round the hat until all the rows have been worked.

Finishing

You will now find that pleats have formed all round the raw edge. Working on the wrong side arrange these following Figure 134 so that 8/9 pleats are to one side and 7/9 to the other; then oversew the top of the pleats firmly together. Turn work to right side.

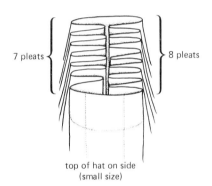

7 pleats

8 pleats

Figure 134

top of hat on side
(small size)

SKIRT WITH SMOCKED PANELS

This skirt has the zip opening set into the centre back seam and two decorative panels of smocking at the front. If it is made in jersey as suggested, the fullness has a graceful slimming effect. The optional sash is a fashion extra worn swathed around the waist or, made shorter and a little wider, becomes a matching scarf.

Materials

250 × 150 cm (2¾ yd × 60 in) fine silky-finish nylon jersey
Skirt placket zip 18 cm (7 in)

back view

Figure 135

Petersham ribbon, thick Vilene or belting to fit waist, 4 cm (1½ in) wide
2 medium-size hooks and eyes

Measurements

As the skirt is full it will fit all sizes and measures approximately 289 cm (114 in) round the hem; waistband, adjustable; length 71 cm (28 in), adjustable.

Cutting out

1 cm (⅜ in) seam allowance has been given on side seams and 2.5 cm (1 in) on centre back seam; 2 cm (¾ in) has been allowed at waistband and 6 cm (2½ in) for hem. Cut two back panels and a centre front panel each 85 × 75 cm (33½ × 29½ in) and two panels for smocking, each 97 × 26 cm (38¼ × 10¼ in). Cut waistband 12 cm (4¾ in) × the length of the waist plus 2 cm (¾ in). From the remainder of the material cut and join sufficient bias strips each 13 cm (5 in) wide to give a length of 282 cm (111 in) for the sash.

Smocking preparation

Make or rule a smocking chart, using any of the methods described for the square cushion on p. 129, to measure 37.5 × 21

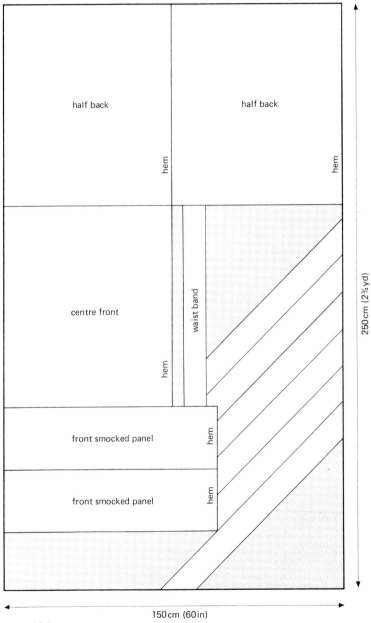

Figure 136

cm (15 × 8 in), with dots or lines 1.5 cm (⅝ in) apart. There
should be 26 dots along the length and 15 dots across the width,
or 25 × 14 squares. The chart should be transferred to the wrong
side of the two smaller panels following Figure 137.

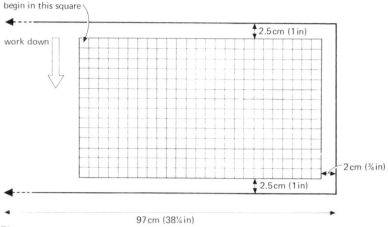

Figure 137

Smocking

Hold the fabric as shown in Figure 137, and begin at the top of
the first row on the left, as indicated. The smocking is worked
across the width and each line, which is adjacent to its neigh-
bour, is formed as described for the square cushion. Continue
until twelve lines have been worked. The final row of dots on the
right end is for help in making up only. Tack pleats resulting
from smocking in place at sides and top of panels.

To make up

Joining panels Taking 1-cm (⅜-in) seam throughout, join the
panels together following Figure 138. Notice that the longer
measurement of the three larger panels runs along the hem and
waistband edges. When joining the smocked panels in place, sew
from the waistband edge so that any unevenness in the length
can be adjusted at the hem. Trim seams to 6 mm (¼ in) and
overcast both raw edges together on each seam.

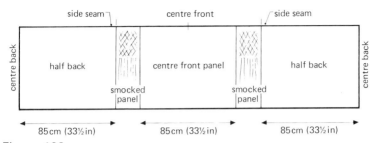

Figure 138

Centre back seam Starting at the waistband edge, tack along the seam line 2.5 cm (1 in) from raw edge for 19 cm (7½ in), then machine stitch the rest of the seam. Snip into the seam allowance just below the tacked portion. Trim and finish the machined remainder of the seam as for the rest of the garment.

Zip opening To set in the zip, press the tacked part of the seam open, pin and tack the closed zip in place with the pull tab 1.5 cm (⅝ in) from the raw edge. Working on the right side, machine or back stitch round the zip 6 mm (¼ in) away from the seam; remove tackings.

Waistband Run two gathering threads along the upper raw edge of the three larger panels 6 mm (¼ in) and 2 cm (¾ in) below it. The easiest way to do this is to loosen the top tension on your machine as much as possible and set the stitch to its longest measurement. Do not gather along the smocked panels. Mark the middle of the centre front panel. Tack 1 cm (⅜ in) to wrong side on both short ends of the waistband and fold the length into four; mark each quarter with a pin. With the right side of the skirt facing, pin and tack the waistband to the work, matching centre front pin to the middle of the front panel and the two other pins to the outer edges of the smocked panels. Draw up gathers to fit and machine stitch. Press waistband up.

Tack stiffening to wrong side of waistband just above the seam, fold remainder of waistband to inside. Turn in seam allowance and slip stitch, but before oversewing short ends, sew corresponding hooks and eyes in place and then slip stitch band over the stitching, so that only the essential parts of the fastenings will show.

Hem Try on skirt and adjust length, levelling the smocked panels if necessary. Overcast the raw edge, turn up hem and slip stitch overcasting to skirt.

Sash Trim joins of sash and overcast, overcast raw edges to neaten.

7

NOVELTIES AND IDEAS

SMOCKED BAG INSET WITH WOODEN BEADS

The smocking on this bag uses vandyke and cable stitches. By picking up alternate dots when gathering, deep pleats are formed which have wooden beads sewn into them when the embroidery is finished. Materials and beads are given for decorating both sides of the bag but one side can be left plain. Assemble the smocked side first and use it as a pattern for cutting the plain side.

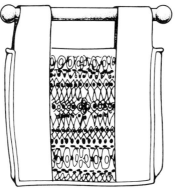

Figure 139   back view (front and back the same)

Materials

100 × 114 cm (1¼ yd × 45 in) fine wool or linen
80 × 91 cm (31½ × 36 in) lining material
Soft embroidery thread skeins, 3 light, 2 medium, 2 dark
2 m (2¼ yd) medium-thickness piping cord

2 smocking transfers 50 × 38 cm (19½ × 15 in) with dots and
rows 8 mm (⅜ in) apart (see p. 38). There should be 37 rows of
49 dots on each transfer, including an extra row at top and
bottom

2 craft rods or lengths of bamboo for handles, approximately 40
cm (16 in) long

5-mm (⅕-in) wooden beads: 64 white, 104 beige, 24 black

3-mm (⅛-in) wooden beads: 76 orange

15-mm (⅗-in) long oval beads: 32 orange

The original uses mid-brown synthetic/wool mix with beige,
apricot and black embroidery

Measurements

Approximately 30 × 30 cm (12 × 12 in), excluding handles, 9
cm (3½ in) deep.

Cutting out

Seam allowance of 1.5 cm (⅝ in) has been given. From wool or
linen material cut two smocking panels each 54 × 40 cm (21½ ×
15¾ in), four side panels each 10 × 58 cm (4 × 23 in), one gusset
12 × 105 cm (4¾ × 41½ in). Lining is cut later.

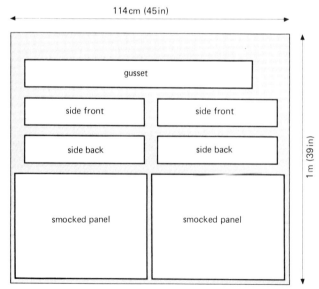

Figure 140

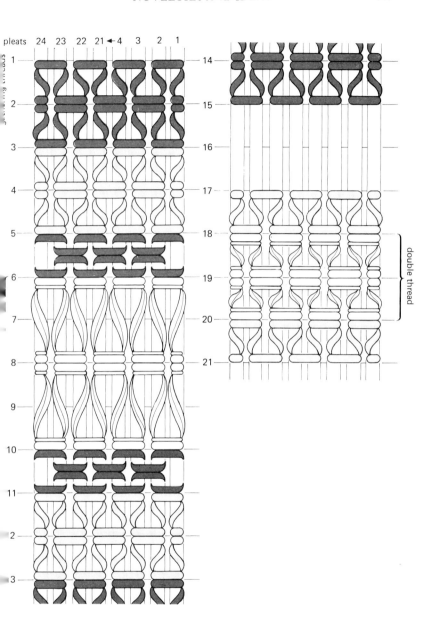

Figure 141

Smocking preparation

Apply the transfers to the wrong side of the panels with a margin of approximately 2 cm (¾ in) all round. Overcast the edges to prevent fraying. If the material will not take the transfer, tack the paper in place and stitch through it. Gather, picking up 25 alternate dots on each row, then draw up threads so that panels measure 10 cm (4 in) across. There will be 24 pleats.

Embroidery

Work the embroidery following Figure 141. The top and bottom row are to help in making up only and are not included. Note that to form complete cells each vandyke row is started and finished over one pleat only. Use double thread on fifth and sixth vandyke rows on top and bottom patterns and on second and third rows on centre pattern. After completing centre pattern, leave two spaces vacant and repeat top pattern. Be sure to make the cable stitches loose as the smocking panel expands when the beads are set in place.

To make up

Withdraw gathering threads. Using sewing thread double, set the beads into the cells formed. Cut two strips of material along the straight grain each 6 cm (2½ in) wide to fit across the top of the smocked panels. With right sides and raw edges together, hand stitch strip to top of smocking tubes on a level with the top row of embroidery; turn strip over to wrong side and catch down. Do not turn in raw edges. Press in 1 cm (⅜ in) down one long edge of each side panel. Hand stitch folded edge to either side of smocked panels in right side, with raw edges level at the bottom. Use the finished pieces to cut lining back and fronts allowing extra for seam on folded and bound edges. Side panels should project 18 cm (7 in) above top edge of smocking and may be trimmed if necessary.

Piping (optional) Cut and join sufficient 4-cm (1½-in) wide bias strips to give a total length of 220 cm (2 yd 10 in), following instructions on pp. 34–5, Neaten one end as shown in Figure 127, fold in half lengthways and tack enclosing piping cord. With raw edges together, tack folded bias to right sides of one assembled piece, beginning and ending level with top of smocked panel.

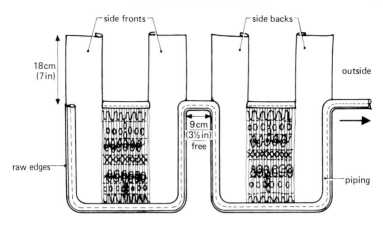

Figure 142

Leave 9 cm (3½ in) free for top of gusset and continue to tack piping to the other piece (see Figure 142). Leave remainder hanging to apply to the other top side of gusset later.

Gusset Press in one short end of gusset to wrong side for 2 cm (¾ in). Working on the wrong side, tack the gusset between the front and back of the bag, starting and ending level with top of smocked panel. Enclose the raw edges of the piping between the gusset and each main piece (Figure 143). Snip into the corners where necessary and machine stitch all round using a piping foot. Turn bag to right side. Slip stitch the pressed-in upper edge

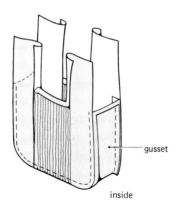

Figure 143

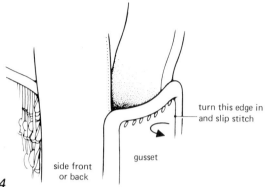

turn this edge in
and slip stitch

gusset

side front
or back

Figure 144

of the gusset below the piping (Figure 144) and fold in the other
short end, trimming if necessary. Trim the piping to fit, turn in
the raw edge and slip stitch to the beginning (see Figure 128).
Stitch the other end of the gusset below the piping.

Lining and handles   Cut a gusset for the lining and assemble as for
the bag, omitting piping. Slip stitch in place. Oversew raw edges
of bag and lining together at the top, fold to inside on a level with
the smocking to form loops for handles. Back stitch loops to
enclose handles, or bore two small holes in each handle under
the loops and use them to stitch handles in place. A bag base
may be made from a piece of hardboard cut to fit, covered in
lining material. Catch the base to the lining on the inside.

A DETACHABLE COLLAR

Use crisp material. The outer edge may be finished with a roll
hem, or narrow lace may be attached with a fine zig-zag stitch.
Taper the ends to meet at centre front. Bind the inner edges and
tie with a bow.

JABOT OR CENTRE FRILL

A high-necked blouse would acquire an expensive air with a frill
like this one made in fine nylon or cotton/polyester material,
which can run down the centre front to the waistline or part of
the way.

NIGHT DRESS

For this design allow 3 m 40 cm × 91 cm material (3¾ yds × 36 in). Across the width cut two strips each 61 × 13 cm (24 × 5 in) for sleeves. Cut remainder in half widthwise for back and front. Iron off smocking transfers about 4–5 cm (1¾–2 in) wide on each piece and join them together, then make narrow hems on each edge of sleeves and on top edge of back and front pieces. Insert gathering threads and smock. Scoop material at underarm and bind armholes, join side seams and finish hem.

BLOUSE OR SMOCK

Allow approximately 2 m 50 cm × 91 cm fabric (2¾ yds by 36 in). Measure round body at underarms and add 5 cm (2 in) for ease. Divide in half to give finished measurements of back and front. Cut two pieces each three times this width by the desired length and smock each across the top to a depth of about 20 cm (8 in) from the shoulder. Ignore neckline shaping for the moment. Cut each sleeve 120 cm (48 in) wide by desired length plus 10 cm (4 in) for the cuff and smock across top edge to a depth of about 10 cm (4 in) from armhole seam. Machine round neckline on back and front and cut out. Join shoulders, bind neck. Join sleeves to armhole edges of front and back and close underarm seams, adding a 10 cm (4 in) square gusset to each. Sew casing for elastic to inside of sleeves at wrists.

SUNTOP

This design is simple, cool and unusual. Measure round the body at underarms and add half as much again, plus a further 25 cm (10 in) for smocking. Work a triangle of smocking at centre front, having the top row 13 cm (5 in) wide. Gather the remainder of the top edge into a band to fit, add straps and trim the edges.

OFF-THE-SHOULDER DRESS

Follow the instructions for the peasant blouse on p. 81, but work a deeper band of smocking and do not bind the neck and shoulder line. At the back of the smocking, stitch herring bone

Figure 146

casing to hold two or three rows of elastic so that the dress will stay securely in place.

SLEEVELESS BLOUSE

Smocking on the shoulders is an attractive but fairly quick way of showing off your embroidery. The finished bands should be approximately 8 cm (3¼ in) wide and deep. Use any blouse pattern for the back. For the front cut a piece of material as wide as the pattern piece plus 32 cm (12½ in). Smock 8 cm (3¼ in) on either side for the shoulders, then machine round the outline of the neck, shoulders and armholes and cut them out. Join shoulders, bind neck and armholes. Dart sides if necessary, close seams and finish lower edges.

BABY'S DRESS

Use the pattern for the baby's dress with bonnet shown on p. 44. Iron off an even number of rows of smocking dots to a depth of about 6 cm (2¼ in) on the front dress only and work honeycomb smocking. Gather sleeves and back without smocking into the neckband. The lower edges of the dress and sleeves may be decorated with bought trimming or embroidery. Try also a patchwork version by cutting the sleeves from another fabric and trimming the bottom of the skirt with a decorative band of the same fabric.

SHOULDER BAG

Embroider decorative smocking all over the front; the back may be left plain. Gather deep pleats on wool/synthetic mixture or needlecord and smock with tapestry wool or a soft embroidery cotton. The bag may be decorated with wooden beads as described on p. 145. To finish join three sides and make two ring carriers from double material each about 13 × 5 cm (5 × 2 in). Thread the carriers through two wooden rings and join them to the top of the bag with the raw edges inside. Add lining and two tassels to the lower corners, then double a length of cord for the handle. Pass the doubled end through one of the rings and pull the ends through the loop. Finish by tying them to the other ring and pull out the ends into tassels.

CUSHIONS

Heart shape

A special anniversary or wedding cushion would make a charming present. If you see polyester satin and stuff without white polyester filling you can wash the complete cushion with removing the padding, thus making your gift completely practical. Embroider or quilt the cushion incorporating names and a date, or sew on bought lace motifs. For the frill, cut a length of fine silk, tulle or plain lace. Make a rolled hem on one edge or sew on narrow lace using a fine zig zag, then work the smocking in one or two pale colours to harmonize with the centre decoration. To finish the cushion add a few narrow ribbon bows at the cleft of the heart.

Oblong

Oblong and square lacey cushions look delightfully luxurious in a bedroom. Sew assorted strips of lace and motifs on to a fine polyester cotton backing. These may be machine made or may be small doilies or odd crochet lace strips found in antique shops. Tucks and satin ribbons can all be used for decorative effect. Either set a band of smocking into the cusion or smock the frills at the ends. It is practical to make up this type of cushion as though it were a pillow slip. It can then be removed easily from its padding for laundering.

LAMPSHADE

This detachable cover may be placed on top of a wire frame which has first been wrapped with bias binding, or it may go over an existing plain pale-coloured shade. Choose fine nylon. Measure round the base of the frame and multiply by three. The length must equal the depth of the frame plus turnings. Iron on enough dots to come about a quarter of the way down the shade, allowing for a 12 mm (½ in) hem at the top. Join the short ends, then hem top and bottom edges. Smock and catch a length of binding or tape to the wrong side of the smocking on the inside. This will ensure that the embroidery does not overstretch with washing so that the shade slips down out of place.

TEA COSY

Make a frill to finish the tea cosy and pick up the colours in the central decoration. To allow the smocking to be seen from either side the frill should be made double. Calculate its desired width and double it, then add on 2.5 cm (1 in) for seam allowance. Measure round the outside of the cosy and multiply by three for the length. Cut out and iron the rows of smocking dots along the length of the strip within 12 mm (½ in) of the raw edges on either side. Work the embroidery, then fold along the length with right sides together and join the short ends. Turn to right side, tack the raw edges together. Sew the frill into the cosy.

TABLE CLOTH

Make this in two pieces. First cut a circle to fit the top of the table plus turnings. Allow three times the diameter of the table top to calculate the finished length of the smocked side and cut this piece three times the required finished length. Smock, then hem the lower edge. Join to the top, which may also be decorated with appliqué or embroidery.

INDEX